MILLER'S
FIELD GUIDE
ART DECO

Consultant: Eric Knowles
Series Editor: Judith Miller

MILLER'S

Miller's Field Guide: Art Deco
Consultant: Eric Knowles

Miller's, a division of Mitchell Beazley,
both imprints of Octopus Publishing Group Ltd
Endeavour House
189 Shaftesbury Avenue
London
WC2H 8JY
www.octopusbooks.co.uk
Miller's is a registered trademark of Octopus Publishing Group Ltd.

Series Editor:	Judith Miller
Publisher:	Alison Starling
Chief Contributor:	Julie Brooke
Editorial Co-ordinator:	Christina Webb
Editorial Assistant:	Fiona Eccles
Proofreader:	Jo Murray
Indexer:	Hilary Bird
Art Director:	Jonathan Christie
Designer:	Ali Scrivens, T J Graphics
Production Controller:	Sarah-Jayne Johnson

ISBN 978 1 84533 950 0

The publishers will be grateful for any information that will assist them in keeping further editions up to date. Although all reasonable care has been taken in the preparation of this book, neither the publishers nor the compilers accept any liability for any consequences arising from the use thereof, nor the information contained herein.

A CIP catalogue record for this book is available from the British Library

Set in Chronicle Deck, Roman, Semibold Italic and Bold
Printed and bound in China

Front cover: A Ferdinand Preiss figure of the "Bat Girl", c1923/24 9.25in (23.5cm) high E
Back cover: A Clarice Cliff 'Orange Roof Cottage' yo vase, (shape 378) c1930 6in (15.5cm) high F
A Trifari 'Jelly Belly' fur-clip, designed by Bel Geddes. 1941 3.25in (8.3cm) long F
Title page: A Clarice Cliff Bizarre 342 'Sunray' vase. 8in (20cm) high F

A marble, gilt bronze and ivory figural group of "The Spring", by Ferdinand Preiss (1892–1943). 6.5in (17cm) high E

Contents

VALUE CODES

Throughout this book the value codes used at the end of each caption correspond to the approximate value of the item. These are broad price ranges and should only be seen as a guide, as prices for antiques vary depending on the condition of the item, geographical location, and market trends. The codes used are as follows:

AAA £100+ ($165,000+)

AA £50–100,000 ($80,000-165,000)

A £25–50,000 ($37,500-80,000)

B £15–25,000 ($22,000-37,500)

C £10–15,000 ($15-22,500)

D £5–10,000 ($7,500-15,000)

E £2–5,000 ($3-7,500)

F £1–2,000 ($1,500-3,000)

G £500–1,000 ($750-1,500)

H under £500 (under $750)

Introduction

Throughout the 1950s and 1960s many dealers and collectors considered little – if anything – of the post-1830 period to be of any merit. With the growing interest worldwide in antiques, the availability of 18thC and 19thC pieces began to dwindle. This led to an increasing demand for artefacts first from the reign of William IV and then from the Victorian period. Eventually, during the 1960s and early 1970s, collectors turned their attention to Art Nouveau, and a few years later they began to recognize the originality of furniture and decorative art objects from the 1920s and 1930s, collectively known as Art Deco.

Pieces from the Art Deco period are sought after not only for their high quality of craftsmanship and inventive forms, but also because they evoke the giddy Twenties – the era of jazz and Hollywood – and the Thirties. New items appeared that reflected the changing lifestyles – such as cocktail glasses and car mascots. Many such pieces display in their decoration a preoccupation with speed and travel. Women came into their own as subjects during this period and are often depicted in decidedly "modern"

A Goldscheider figure of a dancer by Josef Lorenzl. c.1922 18.5in (47cm) high E

clothing or situations – for example, smoking, drinking, or participating in sports, activities that would have seemed almost inconceivable only a few years earlier.

The term Art Deco encompasses two very different styles – the Traditional and the Modern. The Traditionalists, led by the Frenchmen Jacques-Emile Ruhlmann (see pp.14–17) and Jean Dunand (see pp.24–5), adapted and embellished 18thC designs, using exotic woods and materials, and with an emphasis on comfort. The Modernists, such as Ludwig Mies van der Rohe (see pp.26–7) and the British firm of Isokon, advocated clean profiles, machine-made materials, and mass-production. Although the Traditionalist pieces mostly belong to the 1920s and the Modernist to the 1930s, both styles are evident throughout the period.

Craftsman-made pieces, such as the glasswares of Maurice Marinot (see p.57) and the jewellery of Jean Fouquet (see p.189), are hard to come by and can be prohibitively expensive for many collectors. However, the mass-produced hand-finished wares are more readily available and more affordable.

The *Art Deco Field Guide* is a complete sourcebook of the major craftsmen, factories, and styles of the period. Its purpose is to teach how to recognize and assess individual pieces, and provide useful background information on the makers and media. The rest of the work you must do yourself. There is no substitute for first-hand experience: attend auctions and study pieces in museums. Collecting is a matter of experience and confidence. With the help of this book you will quickly find yourself able to make informed judgements, and with this will come the excitement and fun of knowledgeable collecting.

A bronze fish sculpture by Georges Lavroff.
c.1925 15.5in (39.5cm) high E

The Paris Exhibition and the Liner SS *Normandie*

The Art Deco style is firmly associated with two "showcases" – the Paris Exhibition of 1925 and the liner SS *Normandie*, launched in 1935.

The Paris Exhibition – the Exposition des Arts Decoratifs et Industriels Modernes was originally intended to be held some ten years earlier, but was delayed because of the First World War. Encouraged by the French government, which was hoping it would generate trade, the Exhibition was a huge extravaganza. Designers from other countries, in particular the United States, and to a lesser extent

"Normandie" poster, by Cassandre (Adolphe Jean-Marie). 1935 38.25in (97cm) high E

A Paul Kiss wrought-iron guéridon. *25in (63.5cm) diam F*

Britain, were inspired by the event and emulated many of the styles and motifs on display.

Although officially international, the Exhibition was dominated by the leading French craftsmen of the day, such as René Lalique (see pp.50–5) – who designed for the event a 50ft (15m) internally lit glass fountain and waterfall – and master *ébéniste*, Jacques-Emile Ruhlmann (see pp.14–17), who designed the central pavilion, named the "Pavilion for a Rich Collector". Each of the major department stores, such as the Galeries Lafayette and Printemps, had their own specially designed pavilion. Most of the exhibits, and the rooms that housed them, were exotic and relatively traditional. The public were not yet ready for the creations of such craftsmen as Ludwig Mies van der Rohe (see pp.26–7), whose Modernist, minimalist design for one of the pavilions caused such dismay among the Exhibition's organizers that they wished to build a 12ft (3.5m) wall around it. Such avant-garde schemes, which many people today regard as the epitome of the Art Deco style, were not widely adopted until the 1930s.

The SS *Normandie* was launched in 1935. Once again, the top craftsmen of the day were called in to furnish the liner, which became the floating embodiment of the Art Deco style: lighting fixtures were designed by

A c.1920s Georg Jensen silver candelabra, design no. 324. 9in (23cm) high D

Marius-Ernest Sabino (see pp.68–9) and René Lalique, who was also responsible for the wall panels and glass tableware; murals were by Jean Dunand (see pp.24–5), Jean Dupas, and Paul Jouve; furniture was by Jules Leleu and Alavoine, among others; wrought ironwork was by Raymond Subes (see pp.166–7), and the ceramic tiles for the bathrooms were by Jean Mayadon. Other ocean liners were furnished in a similarly luxurious and "modern" style – for example, SS *L'Atlantique*.

FURNITURE

Changing lifestyles after the First World War resulted in a demand for new types of furniture, such as elaborate dressing tables and cocktail cabinets. As luxury items, these were expected to be decorative as well as functional. Mass-production was made possible by technological developments, and many designers experimented with materials not previously used for furniture, such as tubular steel and glass. However, these innovations were carried out alongside the production of traditional types of furniture.

French pieces from the 1920s typify the more opulent style of Art Deco furniture. Designers such as Jacques-Emile Ruhlmann (see pp.14–17) created expensive pieces for the nouveau riche elite. Forms were Traditionalist, based on the late 18thC and early 19thC Directoire period. Upholstery was luxurious, incorporating colourful fabrics.

Wood veneers began to be replaced by polished and figured marble, and luxury woods, such as amboyna and macassar ebony, were also used. Late Traditionalist work, such as that of Jules Leleu and Jean Dunand (see pp.24–5) made extensive use of lacquered surfaces. Süe et Mare (see pp.22–3) exemplify the high watermark of Deco furniture. Its neo-traditionalist forms incorporate vibrant decorative motifs, often in ivory and mother-of-pearl, which elevate utilitarian furniture to the status of art objects. Armand Albert Rateau's furniture, also created for an elite market, is characterized by its use of metal, especially patinated bronze, which was used on indoor furniture for the first time.

By 1925 this extravagant fashion had reached a peak: from then on traditional forms began to be supplanted by the Modernist creations advocated by Le Corbusier and the Bauhaus. Even Ruhlmann eventually incorporated chromed tubular steel into his exotic macassar ebony veneered creations. Other innovative materials, such as plate glass, were promoted by René Lalique (see pp.50–5), who produced panels for furniture, and by master wrought ironworkers, such as Edgar Brandt (see pp.164–5). Formalized flowers gradually gave way to Cubist decoration, and other decorative elements, including those from Egyptian, Aztec, and African art.

In contrast, very little British furniture from the 1930s is Modernist in style. Among the most successful is that by Betty Joel (see pp.40–1), with

A Jacques-Emile Ruhlmann mahogany armchair.
1920 22in (56cm) wide B

A Paul Frankl walnut sofa, with nickelled brass mounts, designed 1933. 72in (183cm) wide D

its emphasis on form and wood grain. Utility is paramount; pieces have a sculptural, balanced quality. Most of the 1930s furniture available in Britain today is by less distinguished designers. Forms were simple, with an emphasis on the craftsmanship necessary to produce an unfussy design. Pale woods, such as sycamore and burr walnut, were popular, and the wood grain was often used as the main decorative element. Oak continued to be used, following traditional construction methods.

The German Bauhaus, which included several important designers, among whom were Walter Gropius,

Marcel Breuer (see pp.28–9), Ludwig Mies van der Rohe (see pp.26–7), and Marianne Brandt, constituted a gathering together of architects and industrial designers who aimed to apply functionalism and minimalism to their work, rather than approaching furniture design from an applied arts point of view. They experimented with new and unusual materials such as concrete, tubular steel, and plate glass. Nothing escaped their influence or treatment; their design principles extended from buildings to canteen cutlery. Any Bauhaus furniture commands a premium. Most items carry a designer's monogram; there is no Bauhaus mark. After the Nazis disbanded the organization on the grounds that it was subversive, many of its members, including Gropius and Mies van der Rohe, moved to the United States where their work was widely accepted.

American designers followed the lead of their European counterparts and used the grain of the wood as a form of decoration, sometimes contrasting it with chrome detailing. A few painted or lacquered pieces of furniture, often edging pieces with primary colours. Pieces are large, as houses had interiors that could accommodate them; the Skyscraper style (see pp.31–2) was created to suit the smaller urban interiors. The concern for functionalism was pioneered by Frank Lloyd Wright (see pp.38–9).

Although many of the finest Art Deco furniture has remained in Paris, good-quality pieces do appear in some sales in Britain and the United States. Consult contemporary journals and periodicals such as *The Studio*: these offer the most useful illustrations, often never seen elsewhere.

A pair of Betty Joel bookcases, in Australian silky oak. c.1934 36in (91.5cm) wide F

Jacques-Emile Ruhlmann

A Ruhlmann ivory inlaid
rosewood cabinet.
c.1919 50.75in (129cm) wide A

1. Does the piece exhibit superior construction and craftsmanship?
2. Are the materials exotic and expensive?
3. Is the form simple, elegant, and balanced?
4. Does the piece have discreet ivory embellishments?
5. Is the decoration subtle?
6. If the item is small is it supported on tapering, slender legs?
7. Are all the joints of the construction completely covered, with surface joints used for decorative purposes only?
8. Is there a branded signature?

Jacques-Emile Ruhlmann (French, 1879–1933)

Initially a painter, Ruhlmann became the best-known French cabinet-maker of his day, following the tradition of the 18thC *ébénistes*. He designed for a rich and exclusive clientele, using exotic woods and other expensive materials. After the First World War he took over his father's successful building firm, Ruhlmann et Laurent, and expanded it with workshops devoted to furniture and other aspects of interior design.

As well as designing a wide range of furniture, including dining tables and chairs, beds, desks, secretaries, mirrors, upholstered armchairs, and so on, Ruhlmann designed all manner of other items for interiors including textiles, light fixtures, and even wastepaper baskets. Ruhlmann's designs were mostly executed by craftsmen at his workshops, rather than by him personally.

Stylistic development

Many of Ruhlmann's most classic Art Deco pieces were produced before 1920. Until the later part of the 1920s his work was in the Traditionalist Art Deco style, based on simplified French Neo-classical designs and always in wood. After 1925 his designs became more Cubist and less symmetrical, although always with a traditional concern for

A Ruhlmann burr amboyna armchair, with ebony details. 1913 27in (68.5cm) wide B

A rare Ruhlmann "Ventru" sideboard, with ivory marquetry. 1929 33in (84cm) high A

Collecting

Ruhlmann's work is regarded as the best of the period. Although pieces turn up fairly regularly at auction, prices are among the highest of any paid for Art Deco furniture – as they were when they were made.

Woods

Macassar ebony was one of Ruhlmann's favourite exotic veneers, along with amboyna elegance and quality. He then began to incorporate some functional metal components, and later, during the 1930s, made more widespread use of metal, tubular steel, and plastic.

Recognition points

- On a number of Ruhlmann pieces, the legs appear to emanate from outside the structure rather than supporting it from underneath.
- Drawered pieces are characterized by the smooth action and snug fit of the drawers.

A Ruhlmann "Elephant" chair, designed 1926. 37in (94cm) wide C

and shagreen. For contrast, he often combined these woods with ivory escutcheons and handles (as in the cabinet on p.14), or with decoration in mother-of-pearl or tortoiseshell.

Many Ruhlmann pieces were made to individual commission. The characteristically heavy forms are relieved by the use of wood grain for decorative effect. Ruhlmann furniture is handmade. The joints are often carefully concealed – for example, any dovetailing on drawers, if visible at all, is very discreet.

Marks

All Ruhlmann's work has a branded signature, "RUHLMANN", in letters ⅓in (1cm) high, followed by the letter A, B, or C, indicating from which of the three ateliers the piece emanated. A is considered the most desirable. Sometimes, only one piece from a suite bears a signature.

After his death, his nephew, Alfred Porteneuve, took over the workshops and repeated some of Ruhlmann's designs, branded "PORTENEUVE". These designs are regarded as of lesser significance.

A rare Ruhlmann black lacquer and glass table. c.1934 31.5in (80cm) wide A

Paul Follot

A Follot bergère *chair, with
ebonized fluted feet. c.1920
32in (81cm) high D*

1. Has the piece been designed with a traditional attention to comfort?
2. On upholstered furniture, is the upholstery part of the main decorative focus?
3. Does the piece exhibit a high level of craftsmanship?
4. On unupholstered pieces, is the emphasis on form, as much as, or more than on decoration?
5. Is the form balanced?
6. Is there any carved floral decoration or inlay work?
7. Do even the heavy pieces look relatively lightweight and elegant?
8. Does the piece use pale-coloured woods, possibly lacquered or gilt?

A Follot sofa. c.1925
63in (160cm) wide B

Paul Follot (French, 1877–1941)

Follot was an interior designer, and as well as furniture, designed textiles, wallpaper, ceramics, and silverware.

Early work

Follot's early work, produced before the mid-1920s, was based on late 18thC forms, with an emphasis on comfort.

A Follot amboyna cabinet, with ivory handles and inlay. c.1925 60.25in (153cm) wide C

A Follot giltwood footstool. c.1920 25in (63.5cm) wide D

A pair of upholstered chairs by Follot. c.1925 A

Some pieces from this period featured giltwood frames with bright upholstery. He preferred to design complete interiors or sets of furniture, and a sofa or chair might be part of a set that included a chaise-longue, three armless chairs, and a small table.

Designs tend to be restrained, with controlled embellishment and an emphasis on simple forms. The plain upholstery would not distract the eye. Floral decoration became gradually more stylized as his career progressed, and was later dispensed with in favour of inlaid decoration.

Recognition point

A carved budding rose, known today as "Follot rose", is often found on Follot's work, especially on back rails and chair splats.

Note

Collectors of Follot should try to familiarize themselves with the full range of his furniture, as, perhaps more with Follot than any other craftsman of the period, his pieces covered the entire style spectrum, ranging from distinctly traditional, like the chair on p.18, to high Art Deco as in the cabinet shown on p.19.

In Follot's case, a field guide can provide only a guideline to his work.

Collecting

The slightly less avant-garde designs are the most readily available. Pieces are seldom signed.

Even the more Modernist end of the spectrum of Follot's work was made from lacquered wood, rather than one of the "new" materials such as amboyna or macassar ebony. Not all his Modernist works date from a later period – some from the pre-war era seem to anticipate the move towards more streamlined, innovative forms that occurred in the early 1930s. Although Follot's designs became increasingly geometric or Cubist, he never followed the route towards functionalism, and his furniture was clearly intended to be comfortable as well as fashionable and attractive. Follot eschewed modern materials, developing instead a growing interest in the possibilities of wood. He

A Follot macassar ebony and rosewood chair, with acorn back. c.1922 20in (51cm) wide D

began by experimenting with inlays, gilding, veneers, and lacquer, and then became increasingly preoccupied with bringing out the contrasts between different woods.

A wooden clock by Follot, carved with a leaf pattern. c.1925 18.5in (47cm) wide E

Louis Süe and André Mare

A Süe et Mare mahogany armoire. c.1918–20 80in (203cm) high D

1. Is the form essentially traditional, and perhaps curvaceous?
2. Is seating furniture comfortable and luxurious?
3. Is the quality of craftsmanship high – for example, are any fixtures ormolu, and well cast?
4. Does the piece make use of exotic veneers or elaborate inlays?
5. Is it large with a solid appearance?
6. Are any feet relatively stylized or elaborately decorated?
7. Are there unusual touches that are superfluous to the structure?

Süe et Mare (French, 1919–28)

Louis Süe and André Mare, both established French designers, set up their "Compagnie des Arts Français" in 1919. The company soon became known by their combined surnames, and its work epitomizes the opulence of French high Art Deco style. It made a range of furniture and designed interiors, using a team of prominent designers, including Maurice Marinot, Pierre Poisson, and André Vera. As well as wood furniture, it produced some in wrought iron, and a number of decorative objects, including lamps, mirror frames, and chandeliers, using stylized natural forms.

Forms and styles

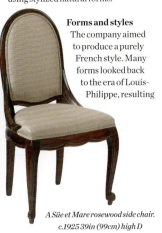

The company aimed to produce a purely French style. Many forms looked back to the era of Louis-Philippe, resulting

A Süe et Mare rosewood side chair. c.1925 39in (99cm) high D

in furniture that is comfortable and luxurious, and often almost Baroque in its extravagance. Many pieces are of massive proportions, with traditional forms relieved by intricate decoration, such as inlays, often in pale woods, and sometimes including mother-of-pearl. Süe et Mare features include:

- scrolled feet
- ormolu fittings
- curved elements in the construction
- the use of veneers to relieve a heavy form
- a delicate scalloped frieze around the top.

Recognition point
- Many Süe et Mare commodes and tables have marble-slab tops.

Later work
In 1928 the designer Jacques Adnet took over the direction of the company and it turned away from the sumptuous style and towards Modernism and the increased use of metal.

Copies
A few lesser French companies copied the work of Süe et Mare. However, these pieces are never of the same quality.

Marks
The furniture is unmarked: the style was considered a sufficient trademark.

Jean Dunand

A lacquered and gilded "La Conquète du Cheval" panel by Dunand. c.1935 24.5in (62cm) high A

1. Is the decoration in metalwork – for example, patinated bronze, or silver inlay, or, alternatively, in very high-quality lacquer, possibly combined with eggshell?

2. Is the work richly made, with expensive materials and a high level of craftsmanship?

3. Is the surface highly polished?

4. Is there an element of Oriental or African influence in the colours or subject matter?

5. Is the piece relatively simple in shape, but with lavish surface decoration?

6. Is there an incised signature? (Bear in mind that not all Dunand's works are signed.)

Jean Dunand (Swiss/French, 1877–1942)

Dunand, who moved to Paris in 1896, was a prolific metalworker, lacquerist, and furniture designer who produced expensive high-quality pieces for the most exclusive end of the market; all pieces were handmade and many were specially commissioned. In 1912 he learned the lacquerwork for which he became best known. His early work featured naturalistic designs, but in common with many craftsmen working at this time, his style became progressively more geometric.

Dunand often worked in metal and was particularly interested in dinanderie – a technique of applying patinated enamelling over a non-precious metal, such as copper or steel. The screens tend to have sharp angular lines and a geometrical bias. Red and black was a favourite combination on vases.

Recognition points

- A Japanese influence is often apparent.
- Dunand often applied lacquerwork to his screens and panels.
- Eggshell was often used on both inner and outer surfaces to give a textured effect.

Note

Dunand used many styles in his career,

A 1920s Dunand lacquered brass vase. 8.5in (21.5cm) high D

and his naturalistic work, which shows a close attention to realistic detail, is very different from his geometric designs, which are highly stylized.

The questions in this *Field Guide* should therefore be regarded as general identification guidelines only, and collectors should familiarize themselves with the full range of Dunand's work.

Marks

Not all Dunand's work is signed. However, some pieces are marked "JEAN DUNAND", sometimes with a serial number. Others have the words "JEAN DUNAND 72 RUE HALLE PARIS MADE IN FRANCE".

Ludwig Mies van der Rohe

A Mies van der Rohe "Barcelona" chair, for Knoll
Associates. 1929 29.5in (75cm) high E

1. Is the base structure in chromed tubular steel?
2. Are the design and construction reduced to simple elements?
3. Does the form follow the function?
4. Does the piece have clarity and elegance of line?
5. In the case of a chair, is it cantilevered, possibly on X-stretchers, without feet?
6. Does any upholstery contribute visually to the structure as well as providing a degree of comfort?
7. Is the piece highly finished, with attention to detail?

Ludwig Mies van der Rohe (German/American, 1886–1969)

In both his glass skyscraper architecture and his furniture design, Mies van der Rohe is the doyen of Modernism. He was one of the chief promoters of the Bauhaus machine-age philosophy. In 1938 he emigrated to the United States and in 1944 he became an American citizen.

From 1927 to 1931 his furniture was produced by the small firm of Berliner Metallgewerbe Josef Müller. Thereafter it was made by Bamberger Metalwerkstätten, and marketing was handled by Thonet-Mundus.

In his furniture designs Mies van der Rohe combines classical forms with Modernism. He achieves a machine-made look but with careful hand-finishing and close attention to detail.

Identification

All Mies van der Rohe's pieces were made by machine rather than by hand, and are not stamped. Many are still in production, although with minor changes to the designs. If in doubt, consult contemporary catalogues for information on design and construction.

The "Barcelona" chair

The "Barcelona" chair (see opposite), was first exhibited in 1929, and is one of the most popular of all 20thC chair designs. It was not mass-produced until after the Second World War but has been in continuous production since (recently by Knoll Associates).

One way to distinguish between early examples and later mass-produced models is from the construction: the top rail of the original was in bent chromed flat steel, with separate sections joined by lap joints and screwed with chrome-headed bolts. Leather straps gave additional support and comfort. In later versions, the top rail is in cut and welded stainless steel. Most retain their original upholstery.

Collecting

Original furniture dating back to Mies van der Rohe's time at the Bauhaus, and before mass-production began, fetches very high prices – as much as ten times that of the later models – particularly in the case of classics such as the "Barcelona" chair.

Mies van der Rohe's famous cantilevered tubular designs first went into production in 1927. These designs included an armchair made of chrome-plated steel tubes. It had a leather seat laced on the underside and the back was held in place with a metal strip and screws. Similar versions exist without arms. Also in this range of cantilevered tubular furniture were steel coffee tables and stools with a leather-sling top.

Marcel Breuer

An early Breuer/Isokon laminated plywood long chair. 1935 45in (114.5cm) wide E

1. Does it contain tubular steel, laminated wood, or aluminium?
2. Does the form follow the function?
3. Are the contours simple?
4. Does the piece make any concessions to comfort, perhaps through a careful balance between a soft seat and a hard frame?
5. If the piece is metal, is it light in look and weight, perhaps with an additional transparent quality?
6. If an upright chair, does the seat appear to float, suspended between the structural elements?
7. Are there any cantilevered elements (after 1923)?

Marcel Breuer (Hungarian, 1902–81)
Breuer moved from Hungary to the Bauhaus in Weimar in 1920. Some of his designs were manufactured in England by PEL, and by Thonet in Austria from 1928. He worked briefly for Isokon in England in 1936. In 1937 he joined his ex-colleague Walter Gropius in the United States. His laminated furniture shares design affinities with that of the Finnish designer, Alvar Aalto.

In many of his designs, the floating impression of the seat and the apparently unsupported arms are typical. Often, a degree of comfort has been sacrificed for functionalist form.

Materials and styles
Breuer revolutionized utility furniture, promoting the use of tubular steel, plywood, and aluminium. He made desks, cabinets, tables, and folding or stacking pieces, and designed furniture for specific interiors.

From the early 1920s Breuer experimented with plywood. With its cantilevered construction, this furniture is typical of the period.

By c.1925, inspired by his new bicycle, Breuer recognized the potential of tubular steel. Initially rough, the steel became more refined over the years and designs were continually updated.

In 1932 Breuer produced his first aluminium furniture. Designs tended to have more curves than the tubular steel furniture. In 1936 Breuer adapted some of his earlier designs to plywood.

Attribution
Breuer's work is not signed or stamped, although Thonet and DIM designs have labels. Attribution can be ascertained by consulting contemporary catalogues.

Recognition point
Runners, instead of feet, were used on chairs and tables after 1925, and contribute to the impression his tubular steel furniture was made in one piece.

Reproductions
Modern reproductions exist but they lack the signs of wear of the originals.

A Breuer/Thonet tubular steel chair, designed 1928–9. 34in (86.5cm) high E

Paul Frankl

A 1930s Frankl streamline sofa and pair of end tables, in black lacquer and leather. 88in (224cm) long C

1. Is the piece elegant in style, showing a strong architectural influence?
2. Is the design reminiscent of skyscrapers in particular?
3. Is there an element of novelty in the design?
4. Is the surface lacquered, with metal or Bakelite inlays or fittings?
5. Is there very little surface decoration?
6. Is any trim red and black in colour, with a turquoise, blue, or green interior?
7. Does it use pale-coloured American woods, such as birch or maple?
8. Does the piece have a named metal tag?

Paul T. Frankl (Austrian/American, 1886–1958)

Born in Austria, Frankl emigrated to the United States during the First World War. He was one of the USA's pioneer Modernists and the first furniture designer to reflect contemporary architecture, a result of his early training in architecture and engineering. In the late 1920s he wrote five books and a number of influential articles on form and design.

A Paul Frankl Skyscraper chest, designed c.1925–7. 56in (142cm) high D

Frankl's early work, from before 1920, is relatively undistinguished and European in style, in accordance with the tastes of his fashionable American clientele. Later work, from 1925 onwards, is more individual and thus more collectable.

There is an element of novelty about all Frankl pieces. His designs place an emphasis on geometry, and their sometimes severe outlines are almost Neo-Biedermeier in style.

Frankl furniture from the early 1920s favours oak and metal, often with ebonized frames.

Skyscraper furniture

Frankl is perhaps best known for his range of Skyscraper furniture (see left). This style, which he pioneered in 1925 and continued working in until 1930, showed an awareness of the needs of smaller, urban spaces. The name evokes New York's remarkable Art Deco architecture, and was used by Frankl as a trademark.

Many of the pieces are multi-functional and combine cupboards, display units, and bookcases. They are frequently made of California redwood, usually with a red, silver, or black lacquered trim. The interiors are in turquoise, blue, or green, and many of these pieces have plastic or metallic finishes.

Check the condition of lacquering and metallic paint, which are easily marked or scratched. A small degree of wear is to be expected, and is acceptable to collectors provided the decoration has not worn away completely.

Skyscraper furniture is often simple in appearance, with pure uncluttered lines. This chest (see p.31) is typical in its rectilinear, pyramidal form, scant decoration, and simple construction.

- The standard of cabinetry on Skyscraper pieces is usually poor. They have not been commercially reproduced, but modern copies do exist.
- Other American designers, such as Kem Weber, Abel Faidy, Norman Bel

Geddes (see pp.170–1), and J. B. Peters, also adopted the Skyscraper form, in other media as well as furniture. Their work is less collectable, so check that pieces bear the Frankl mark – a metal tag, stamped "Skyscraper Furniture, Frankl Galleries, 4 East 48th Street, New York".

Frankl's "Chinese" chair from c.1930, has a contrasted red and black lacquering and gold detailing, and reflects his interest in the Orient and Oriental styles, following a trip to the Far East early in the 1920s. Sets in this style are hard to come by. Furniture of this type complemented the highly popular Chinese style of 1930s fashionable interior design.

- Like the Skyscraper examples, Frankl's other furniture from the late 1920s is in wood with brightly coloured lacquered and painted surfaces, often in red and black.
- In this period Frankl exploited the design potential of mirrored glass, often using it for the tops of pieces, together with Bakelite and metal fittings, giving a decidedly theatrical effect.
- Pieces from this period are usually innovative in style, and are highly collectable and desirable.

A 1930s Frankl chrome and black lacquer console table. 27in (68.5cm) wide C

Later work

After 1930 Frankl turned his back on the Skyscraper furniture concept and concentrated instead on metal furnishings, producing tubular chromed chairs and consoles and Formica-topped metal tables. In keeping with the idea of the period, these meet with strict standards of functionalism, and can be compared with the work of Donald Deskey (see pp.34–7).

In the 1930s Frankl also produced an innovative range of sun parlour and patio seat furniture in wicker and other cane fibres, reviving a popular Victorian style but adding angular corners and armrests in keeping with the spirit of Modernism.

A Frankl painted wood dressing table, with a mirrored surface. c.1925 44in (112cm) wide D

A c.1940s Frankl coffee table, in red and black lacquer. 22.5in (57cm) high D

A Frankl "D" chair, in black lacquer and black vinyl upholstery with red piping. c.1927 26.5in (67.5cm) high E

Donald Deskey

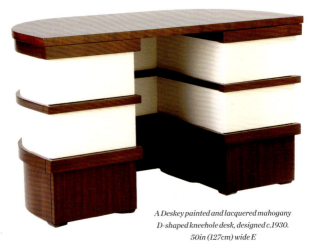

*A Deskey painted and lacquered mahogany
D-shaped kneehole desk, designed c.1930.
50in (127cm) wide E*

1. Are forms based on rectilinear lines and geometry, with a complete absence of ornament?
2. If furniture, does the item incorporate bold colour contrasts, such as a metal or metallic surface with a primary colour?
3. Is there any evidence of the designer's attention to simplicity and economy of construction?
4. Does the item have the appearance of an "industrial prototype"?
5. Are any of the materials extremely unusual and possibly unprecedented?
6. Does the item show a particularly high standard of construction?

Donald Deskey (American, 1894–1989)

By the late 1920s Deskey, who began his career in an advertising agency, had achieved recognition as a furniture and product designer. He combined a taste for functionalism with a uniquely American flair and mastery of the "streamlined" style. His work for private commissions was of unique design and rarely appears on the market today.

Deskey-Vollmer

Most Deskey pieces found today were produced between 1927 and 1931 with Deskey's business partner Phillip Vollmer. These were designed to be economically manufactured on an industrial scale, although many were ultimately produced in small quantities. Tables, seating, small desks, chests, and a range of innovative lighting devices were made in brushed or chromium-plated steel in bent form, tubular steel, and plate glass, often coloured, which gave them a "Bauhaus" look. Aluminium, Bakelite, and cork were also used.

Commissioned products

In the late 1920s Deskey worked in collaboration with Frankl (see pp. 30–3), and on commission for several American manufacturers, including Eskey, Amodec, and the firm of Schmieg-Hungate & Kotzian (all New York-based firms). Most of this was wood-veneered furniture of more conventional design than the Deskey-Vollmer products, and tends to be less collectable today. Finishes include macassar ebony, sometimes in combination with brass, and a variety of blond woods, as well as some painted surfaces. Commissioned work also included designs for entire interiors.

A 1930s Deskey-Vollmer aluminium and black laminate floor lamp.

18in (46cm) diam C

A Deskey painted mahogany four-drawer dresser, designed c.1930s. 72in (183cm) high E

Marks

Despite going on to design corporate marks for companies such as Incoterm Corporation, Aqua Velva, and Yardley of London, the majority of Deskey's furniture is unsigned, although most designs are recorded in modern publications. Small items and lighting are rarely signed, but some furniture bears Deskey-Vollmer tags, and other manufacturers used their own stamps or tags, although these do not always credit Deskey as the designer. Unsigned pieces will therefore require research.

A Deskey Radio City Music Hall sofa c.1932 72in (183cm) long B

A Deskey side table, with black glass top on chromed steel base, designed c.1927. 22.25in (56.5cm) wide E

of his designs are characterized by the use of luxurious materials including exotic woods, often edged in silver leaf, with silk or calf skin upholstery. They may feature wood veneers and parquetry or subtle carved details. Products were small-scale, extremely elegant, and of high quality.

In the 1930s he designed furniture for the retailer Schmieg & Kotzian (which also traded as Schmieg-Hungate & Kotzian), which was renowned for its handmade reproductions of 18thC furniture. The company's label may be found on his work. At this time, he also created avant-garde glass and nickel furniture. Most items are made to high standards of craftsmanship and many are specially commissioned.

Eugene Schoen (American, 1880–1957)

Schoen set up an architectural practice in New York in 1905, but he also worked as an interior designer and art-gallery owner from c.1920 until the Second World War. He was particularly influenced by French furniture and many

A cross-hatched parquetry chest, designed by Schoen for Schmieg-Hungate & Kotzian. c.1935 45in (114.5cm) wide C

Frank Lloyd Wright

1. Is the form rectilinear, with an architectural influence?
2. Is the piece functional rather than decorative?
3. Are any decorative elements incorporated into the form, rather than being added to the surface?
4. If it is all wood, does it have a solid, chunky appearance?
5. If the piece is a chair, is it comparatively high-backed?
6. Does it sacrifice a degree of comfort for visual appearance?
7. Is the use of any colour dramatic, perhaps just one or two colours applied in simple blocks?

A Lloyd Wright Price Tower Executive chair.
1956 36in (91.5cm) high C

Frank Lloyd Wright (American, 1867–1959)

The foremost exponent of the Prairie School, an American Modernist movement in domestic architecture established c.1895, Frank Lloyd Wright's furniture shows an unmistakeably architectural influence; indeed, some pieces, such as the desks and chairs made for the S. C. Johnson Administration building in Wisconsin, USA, were designed to reflect the interior and exterior architecture of a specific building.

Wright designed furniture from the end of the 19thC until the middle of the 20thC, but pieces are usually fairly easy to date: furniture of the 1920s retains an Arts and Crafts/Art Nouveau feel, although the form is almost always innovative. Most pieces are in wood, usually oak, and often handmade. In the 1920s shapes and motifs are commonly Cubistic or angular, many reflecting a Mayan, Aztec, or Japanese influence.

During the 1930s, designs become progressively more functional and utilitarian, with decoration kept to a minimum, usually as an integral part of the form.

By the late 1930s pieces were machine-produced partly or wholly in metal, and designs were becoming progressively more adventurous. Wright returned to wood in the 1950s.

Collecting

As Frank Lloyd Wright is one of the most famous architect/designers of the 20thC, his work commands high prices, especially as many pieces were made to private commission, rather than mass-produced. Unique designs and those made as one of a very limited series inevitably command a premium. The furniture is unsigned, but the provenance of individual pieces is usually well documented. Wright worked in a range of media: he designed copper urns and other decorative metalwares, table lamps, textiles, and ceramics, notably tablewares for the Japanese/American firm Noritake (see p.127). His architectural plates and drawings are also highly collectable. His work is more readily available in the United States than elsewhere.

Fakes

Wright's furniture is not known to have been faked, although there are some honest reproductions, which, unlike the originals, do not have the characteristic signs of wear and tear.

A typical wood chair from c.1920 may be made from oak and functionalist in form with a Japanese influence – for example, the dramatic use of zigzag, and the absence of surface decoration – and employ upholstery to soften a hard form.

Betty Joel

A Joel/Token wild African cherry mahogany kneehole desk. 1935 75in (190.5cm) wide F

1. Is the piece imposing and solid-looking?
2. Are the contours gentle and curved?
3. Is the piece devoid of carving or surface decoration?
4. Is a decorative feature made of the wood grain?
5. Are any fixtures simple and unfussy?
6. Is the piece hand-finished?
7. Is the craftsmanship top quality?
8. Do the drawers fit snugly?
9. Is the piece labelled?

Betty Joel (British, 1896–1984)

Betty Joel was born in China and came to Britain after the First World War. In 1921 she established a furniture workshop in Hayling Island, followed by factories in Portsmouth and Kingston, and a shop in London. Much of her work was commissioned and many pieces are built-in. Betty Joel's furniture is large in size. It is usually practical, and even versatile. Betty Joel designed some unit furniture for the Gordon Russell company (see pp.42–3) in 1934.

Decoration

Designs from the early 1920s are often heavily upholstered and paired with rugs. By the end of the 1920s Joel had developed a more distinctive furniture style, and her 1930s pieces are simpler and more geometric.

Joel furniture is simple and unfussy and usually devoid of carved decoration and painted finishes. Some pieces are lacquered, but she preferred to use the wood grain as the main, or sole decorative element. Alternatively, a decorative effect might be achieved by using contrasting veneers.

Construction

All pieces are hand-finished, although some machinery was used in the construction. The quality of the craftsmanship is excellent.

Materials

Joel used conservatively grained woods, arranged to achieve an almost monochromatic effect. Her furniture from the 1930s uses plywood laminates and other man-made materials.

Form

Form is given priority over decoration, and pieces are strong and solid-looking. Some use is made of geometric and angular shapes, but Joel favoured ellipses and curves.

Handles and drawers

Handles are simple, usually of a grip rather than a hanging type.

Marks

Furniture bears a glazed paper label, which gives the date and signature of the designer and craftsman, and may read "Made at the Token Works, Kingston."

A pair of Joel/Token Queensland silky oak bedside cabinets. 1934 36in (91.5cm) high F

Gordon Russell

A Gordon Russell light oak dressing table, with walnut handles. 1929 50in (127cm) wide F

1. Is the piece handmade with a hand-finished surface?
2. Is the form relatively plain, with an emphasis on careful construction rather than on carving and surface decoration?
3. Is the piece strong and solidly constructed, with all the elements contributing to the structure, including those that also have a decorative value?
4. Is it all wood, with dowel joints and no metal?
5. Are the pegs and other elements of the structure clearly visible?

Gordon Russell (British, 1892–1980)

A member of the Cotswold School of the early 20thC, Russell advocated the use of traditional techniques and never really made the transition to Modernist materials and styles. He made a wide range of items, including dining room, bedroom, and office furniture.

Russell was primarily a designer; it is unlikely that he made many pieces himself. Some furniture comes with a paper label. His Cotswold workshop closed in 2000.

Forms and decoration

Pieces are all handmade, often in oak, with an emphasis on quality of construction. No use is made of carving or other decoration, as the form was considered sufficient in itself. Even those concessions to ornament, such as the ear pieces (the shaped sections

A Gordon Russell side cabinet by David Booth, designed 1950. 47.5in (120.5cm) wide G

between the legs and the frieze) and the spandrels used in the corners of some tables, are primarily functional and only incidentally decorative. The peg construction used is clearly visible.

Condition

Ear pieces are vulnerable to being knocked and damaged. Make sure that they are original by checking that the wood corresponds in colour to the main piece. Collectors should expect to find some wear: this is not detrimental to value unless the damage is severe. Chairs are sometimes reupholstered so it is particularly important to check those with modern springing or modern-looking hide covers for signs of age, as the whole piece may be recent.

Peter Waals (Dutch, 1870–1937)

Another member of the Cotswold School, Waals designed furniture that was quintessentially British. Like that of Russell, his work looks back more to Arts and Crafts and Art Nouveau than forward to Art Deco, although its functional appearance gives it something in common with European Modernist furniture.

Waals preferred country woods, especially walnut, cedar, oak, and limed oak. Pieces are rarely signed, but many are commissioned and so have an available history.

Other furniture

A 1930s Heal's figured walnut stepped side cupboard. 39in (99cm) high G

for example, leather upholstery can crack and veneers may deteriorate (although restoration is sometimes possible).

The best of the less expensive furniture includes bedroom suites, which may comprise a wardrobe, dressing table, and stool, and dining room tables and chairs, along with occasional tables. Light woods command a premium.

Furniture made by UK firm Heal &

Furniture of the 1920s and 1930s is for the most part prohibitively expensive – as it was when first made. This is particularly true of work attributed to the top craftsmen. However, some good-quality furniture, much of it made in emulation of the most popular pieces of the period, is still affordable. Not all of it is worth buying: some pieces are large and clumsy and generally of poor quality. The most successful designs tend to be those of relatively plain form and simple lines, perhaps with the innovative elements combined with attractive supports or clever use of materials. Condition is also a factor. Restoration can be expensive. Some furniture of lesser quality may not have fared well –

A Robert Winthrop Chanler screen, with zebras and stripes. 1928 78in (198cm) high D

Son (1810–present) has an architectural look, with the wood grain as the chief decorative element. Work of the 1930s is more avant-garde, and may combine contemporary and traditional elements.

Harry and Lou Epstein helped to make suite furniture popular in the UK. They made Art Deco-style furniture, mainly in bleached walnut, from the 1930s into the 1950s.

Cocktail cabinets are emblematic of the Jazz Age. Many open to show an illuminated interior, the action of the door raising internal fixtures containing glasses and accessories.

- Biedermeier elements, such as the use of pale woods and an unornamented design, often feature, sometimes to dramatic effect.
- Missing fitments should be reflected in the price. Veneers should be intact.

Pianos from the 1920s and 1930s represent excellent value, especially if they are still in working order (although they nearly always need restringing). The baby grands produced by Eavestaff are of a more saleable size.

Screens are evocative of the Jazz Age and can command high prices, especially if they feature geometric decoration. A number were made in mirrored glass, which was also used for mirror frames, some small occasional tables, and to line cocktail cabinets. In England some rather sombre screens incorporating marquetry and stained wood landscapes were made by Rowley.

Gerald Summers (1899–1967) was one of the few British designers to use innovative forms. He is known for the seating he produced under commission for several British stores.

A 1930s Epstein walnut cocktail cabinet, with a mirrored bar. 64in (162.5cm) high E

A bent birch plywood armchair, by Gerald Summers. 1933–4 23.75in (60.5cm) wide B

GLASS

Art glass, which had declined at the end of the Art Nouveau era, enjoyed a revival in the 1920s and 1930s. During this period artists developed an awareness of the creative potential offered by glass, which was used in a variety of new ways, as a structural as well as a decorative medium. Architects and designers

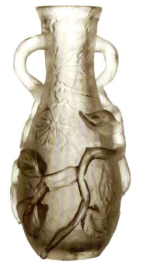

A rare Steuben crystal quartz glass vase, by Frederick Carder. 1930–2 11.5in (29cm) high D

worked imaginatively with plate and mirror glass, and old techniques were adapted to suit new styles. Many of the more ornate items are apparently functional – for example, vases, bowls, and so on – but were intended to be primarily decorative.

The French were the leading innovative glassmakers of the time. Many well-designed pieces were also produced in the United States. British manufacturers produced a large quantity of pseudo-Georgian and pseudo-Victorian glassware alongside more modern articles.

Moulded glass is the most prolific area, and quality varies considerably. The leading artist in this field was René Lalique (see pp.50–5), whose wares were emulated by a number of other glassmakers, including Marius-Ernest Sabino (see p.68), and the firms of Verlys, Barolac, Etling (see p.69), and Valton, all of whom worked in moulded opalescent glass.

The best enamelled glass is by the French artist Marcel Goupy (see pp.70–1), Jean Luce (see p.71), the firms of Baccarat (see p.66), Decuper-Delvaux and Verdar, the Austrian designer Auguste-Claude Heiligenstein, and the Czech factories working in imitation of

A large 1920s orange and yellow enamel Daum bowl. 12.75in (32.5cm) diam E

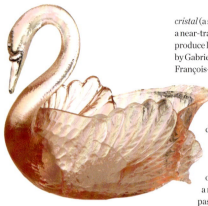

A Cambridge Glass Company Depression glass swan. c.1928 8.5in (21.5cm) long H

Baccarat and Lalique. Enamelled glass is not as common as moulded glass, and can command a higher price.

Engraved glass was made primarily by the Swedish firm Orrefors (see pp.72–3), and the American Steuben Glassworks (see pp.74–5). Major French designers working in the medium were Daum (see pp.58–61), and Maurice Marinot (see p.57). In England engraved glass was produced by Thomas Webb after designs by W. Clyne Farquharson and Keith Murray (see pp.106–7).

The labour-intensive techniques of *pâte-de-verre* (glass paste heated until it fuses within the mould) and *pâte-de-*

cristal (a similar process that achieves a near-transparent effect) were used to produce luxury items. The best pieces are by Gabriel Argy-Rousseau (see pp.62–3), François-Emile Décorchemont (see p.64), Amalric Walter (see p.65) and Frederick Carder (see p.75).

As with furniture, the demand for new forms arose from changes in lifestyle. For example, cocktail parties became the vogue once drinking had become a more socially acceptable pastime. The survival rate of cocktail glasses is poor. Products that became popular during this period include perfume bottles (see p.67) and car mascots, which both provide fruitful areas for collectors.

René Lalique dominated the market, and his vases, tablewares, and car mascots are widely available. He also used glass for light fixtures and in architectural settings. There are many pseudo-Lalique light fixtures on the market: these are of obviously poorer quality, which is reflected in the prices.

There is a type of glass mass-produced during the 1930s in Europe and the United States referred to by the American term "Depression glass", which is angular and frosted in appearance, usually in murky colours, including muted green, peach, or black; it is of simple moulded form. Depression glass consists largely of low-budget domestic wares, including shallow glass bowls with figural decoration, and figurines of tropical fish. It has little artistic or constructional merit. Cloud glass by the Gateshead firm of Davidson has been popular with collectors. This is often dark brown with a random swirling effect.

It is still possible to buy Art Deco glassware at a reasonable price. Decorative vases and bibelots – for example, small glass animals – are the objects most commonly found today. Few glasses have survived: many of those which have are enamelled, often with designs showing cockerels. Enamel wares by Delvaux have not yet acquired a status that makes them prohibitively expensive. Baccarat wares are still relatively underrated. There is also some good Czech glass available, especially the figural types and pieces with hand-engraving or geometric enamelling.

Pâte-de-verre glass was popular in the Art Nouveau and Art Deco periods. It was made from a paste of powdered glass to which coloured glass or metallic oxides were added to provide colour. The mixture was then fired in a mould to give it shape.

The procedure had a fairly high failure rate as the mould could break under heat or the paste fail to gel.

Pâte-de-cristal was a method developed by Gabriel Argy-Rousseau (see pp.62–3) and favoured by Décorchemont (see p.64). It is similar to *pâte-de-verre* but is made by adding an aqueous adhesive before subjecting the mould to an extended firing at a lower temperature; this makes the colour easier to control and results in a translucent, richly coloured vessel.

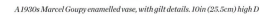

A 1930s Marcel Goupy enamelled vase, with gilt details. 10in (25.5cm) high D

René Lalique

A Lalique "Deux Figurines" clear and frosted glass clock. c.1926 15.25in (39cm) high D

1. Is the piece marked?
2. Is the form inventive?
3. Are the form and decoration harmoniously balanced?
4. Is the style highly individual, and perhaps reminiscent of Art Nouveau, especially in figural work?
5. Is figural work detailed, with precisely rendered facial expressions?
6. Does clear glass have a dark tone compared with modern crystal?

René Lalique (French, 1860–1945)

Lalique, the foremost jeweller of the Art Nouveau period, became the leading glass designer of the Art Deco period, making a wide range of objects, including vases, car mascots, perfume bottles, tablewares, plates, clocks, jewellery, lighting, and figurines. Some of his glass was incorporated into furniture or architecture. Most wares were machine-made for the top end of the mass-market. The perfume bottles were also expensive in their day as they often carried scent by top parfumiers.

Lalique was a prolific designer and his output consisted of an enormous range of items. Pieces with figural subjects are the most popular, followed by insects, animals, geometric motifs, floral wares, and fish.

The 1932 catalogue

The 1932 catalogue of Lalique's wares (since reprinted) is essential to serious collectors as it carries almost the full range of items designed by Lalique, and the dates when they were first made. The catalogue also gives dimensions, but quoted heights should not be regarded as definitive, as proportions do vary between pieces.

Opalescent glass

Most wares are opalescent, produced by adding phosphates, fluorine, and aluminium oxide to the glass to make it opaque, and cobalt to give an internal blue tint. High-relief areas are more opaque than thin-walled parts. (This technique was used by other makers, notably Sabino – see p.68.)

Opalescent glass was

A Lalique "Champagne" vase. c.1927 6.5in (16.5cm) high E

made only during Lalique's lifetime: most of the modern reproductions of original pieces by the Lalique company are in frosted or clear glass.

Condition

Unless the item is exceptionally rare, Lalique pieces must be in pristine condition to be of any great value. Chips can often be removed by grinding and polishing. Scrutinize the overall proportions of the piece as these are sometimes distorted – for example, in smoothing out chipped areas. The bases and rims are often the areas most liable to damage. Acid can be used to disguise the damage by re-frosting glass that was originally frosted. Protruding parts, such as beaks on small birds and fingers on figures, and so on, are also extremely vulnerable.

Genuine pieces will exhibit a faint mould line extending from the rim to the base – beware of pieces where the base is so highly polished that the mould line is not apparent.

Car mascots

Car mascots were made in 29 designs. Birds and animals are common subjects, showing either just the head or the complete creature. Others depict nude female figures.

Mascots are usually in clear and frosted glass, sometimes polished. A few are in clear tinted glass.

The car mascots that come up most frequently for sale are:

- "St Christophe"
- "Archer"
- "Coq Nain" (a cockerel)
- "Perche" (a fish)
- "Grand Libellule" (a dragonfly)
- "Tête d'Aigle" (an eagle's head)
- "Sanglier" (a wild boar)
- "Chrysis" (a kneeling nude)
- "Longchamps" (a horse's head)
- "Cinq Chevaux" (five rearing horses)
- "Tête de Paon" (a peacock's head)
- "Victoire" (a female head)

A René Lalique "Archer" car mascot. c.1926
4.75in (12cm) high E

Perfume bottles

Lalique's earliest scent bottles were commissioned by François Côty. These are usually crisply moulded panel forms; the emphasis is on the decorative stopper.

Later, Lalique produced perfume bottles for many of the top parfumiers, including Molinard and Roger & Gallet. The most inventive forms are in greatest demand, and those with the "tiara" stopper are also very collectable. Many bottles and stoppers were made in a choice of colours.

Sealed bottles with original contents and cartons will always command a premium with collectors. Bottles in solid colours are also desirable. More than one stopper was designed for some bottles – check with the 1932 catalogue (see p.51).

The underside of the stopper should bear a number corresponding to that on the base. Some very small bottles carry the initials "RL" instead of a full signature.

Vases

Lalique created highly decorative vases – he designed more than 200 in the 1920s alone – and many of them are sculptural in form.

The integration of form with decoration is particularly striking in the famous serpent vase, which was issued

Lalique "La Phalene" perfume bottle for D'Heraud. c.1923–9. 3.5in (9cm) high E

in a range of colours, including amber. Typically for Lalique vases, the design is in high relief.

Cire perdue

Glass items, such as the vase shown on p.54, made by the *cire perdue* ("lost wax") method, a casting process that results in unique casts, were the only wares actually made by Lalique, rather than by the workshop to his design. They are thus eagerly sought after, especially as they are unique – the mould has to be broken in order to retrieve the glass. As well as his wheel-cut signature, these wares often carry the last two numerals of the year they were made preceded by a serial number.

Lamps

Lalique made wall lights, chandeliers, ceiling bowls, and table lamps. The lamps often have inventive forms – one is similar to the tiara-stoppered perfume bottle. Others contain figural decoration or have bronze bases.

Tablewares

Like the vases, the tablewares were decorative and practical. The shell bowls were the most popular items. The survival rate of glasses is poor as they were invariably of very thin glass.

Jewellery

Lalique made his name creating extravagant Art Nouveau jewellery. His Art Deco glass jewellery was simpler, but no less eye-catching. Many pieces are in bright colours, such as the electric blue of the pendant opposite (an effect sometimes achieved by using a coloured foil back). Coloured glass is often used in Lalique pieces in preference to precious gemstones.

Marks

Most wares are marked "R Lalique", often with "France" in matching script and a model number. The "L" was sometimes elongated. The signature "R. LALIQUE" was also used. Pieces made after 1950 are signed in script "Lalique France", without the initial "R", which was only used during Lalique's lifetime.

Alterations

Vases may have had their handles removed, while some shell bowls were converted to ceiling bowls, often with non-Lalique glass frosted surrounds, by the Brèves Gallery, which retailed most of the Lalique sold in Britain.

A René Lalique "Huit Serpents" cire perdue
vase. c.1924 8.25in (21cm) high A

Fakes

Lalique glass has been much faked. Modern fakes are very poor. Those made in the 1920s and 1930s are better. Genuine pieces have the form, colour, and style of decoration readily associated with Lalique. The most obvious flaw is often the colour – fakes or copies were made in ones never used by Lalique. Often the rims are too thick.

Many of these fakes bear a wide stencilled mark in relief, with some distance between each letter – not a characteristic of Lalique's marks. The fakes tend to be fairly lightweight. Opalescence, where used, is often all-over, rather than controlled.

A Lalique "Sorbier" pendant. c.1920 2in (5cm) long F

"Perruches" vase by Consolidated Glass Company. 1919 10.25in (26cm) high G

Consolidated Glass Company (American, 1925–c.1960)

The company produced a range of glass called Martele from 1925 to the 1960s. Many pieces were inspired by, and very similar to, Lalique designs. Some pieces were made with two differently coloured layers of glass. The "Perruches" vase (see left) is an almost direct copy of a Lalique piece designed in 1919. The main difference is that the Consolidated version has a slightly flared rim. The additional rim can be polished away and fake marks added.

Charles Schneider

A Schneider acid-etched geometric vase on a pedestal base. c.1925 9in (23cm) high D

1. Is the piece heavily walled and moulded?
2. Is the form conventional and without sculptural quality?
3. Does it have an irregular, trapped bubble effect?
4. Does the decoration appear unintentionally random?
5. Are the decoration and form poorly integrated?
6. Is the signature stencilled?

Charles Schneider Glassworks (French, 1913–81)

Charles Schneider (1881–1953) was inspired by the work of Maurice Marinot and created similar mottled glass using heavily walled moulded forms and an irregular, trapped bubble effect. Pieces were produced in relatively large numbers and so tend to be more affordable than those by Marinot.

Schneider also designed cameo and acid-cut pieces similar to those of Daum Frères and featuring geometric designs or stylized flowers on boldly coloured glass forms. These have been reappraised in recent years and are now no longer considered to be inferior to those by Daum, although the latter are typically more valuable.

Marks

Pieces are signed with the stencilled signature "SCHNEIDER". Many Schneider wares are signed "Le Verre Francais", or "CHARDER".

Schneider also made cameo glass and internally mottled opaque glass, lampshades, and table lamps, some of which resemble work by Daum (see pp.58–61) where he had worked before starting his own glassworks.

Maurice Marinot

1. Is the piece heavy in form?
2. Has the glass been treated as a sculptural medium?
3. Is there an emphasis on internal decoration?
4. Is the design encased in a heavy clear glass surround?
5. Is there an attempt at tightly controlled use of decorative effect?
6. Does the piece have an engraved signature, and a number?

A Marinot bottle with stopper, with enamelled rim. 1910–20 6.25in (16cm) high C

Maurice Marinot (French, 1882–1960)
A technician, chemist, and painter, Marinot became fascinated with glass when he visited a friend's glassworks.

All his glass was hand-made. Many pieces have a clear-grey or pale yellow tint. He was not prolific; consequently his work is relatively hard to find and because of its quality it is expensive.

Decorative techniques
Marinot was primarily interested in the decorative possibilities of glass, especially the way in which imperfections could be turned to decorative advantage. At first he worked with enamels, c.1915–18; he then experimented with bubbles, etching, and wheel carving. He also employed deep acid-cutting, contrasting a polished upper surface and a granular or frosted lower surface. In the early to mid-1920s he shaped the glass at the furnace.

- Even small pieces are heavy in form.
- Stoppers are nearly always in clear glass although they may be given a decorative surface treatment.
- The most successful of the craftsmen who emulated Marinot were Henri Navarre, André Thuret, and Charles Schneider.

Marks
Marinot's work may bear an engraved signature, "Marinot", and be numbered on a paper label attached to the base.

The Daum Factory

A Daum etched and enamelled three-handled vase. 11in (28cm) high B

1. Does the piece make use of all-over decoration?
2. Is the surface grainy and uneven?
3. Is the decoration abstract?
4. Is the form fairly heavy and thick-walled, giving a robust impression?
5. Is it signed, probably on the footrim?

Daum Frères (French, c.1878–present)

During the Art Nouveau period (1890–1914) this leading glassworks produced a large quantity of cameo, or overlay, glass, with the naturalistic motifs typical of the period. During the 1920s and 1930s the output consisted of mainly etched glass, which soon superseded cameo glass in popularity, although the firm continued to make cameo glass throughout the period. Following closure during the First World War, the factory reopened in 1919 under Paul Daum.

The Daum glassworks embraced Art Deco with enthusiasm during the 1920s, and its lamps, bowls, and large decorative vases took an innovative direction. Heavy acid-etched wares with deep decoration predominated. The most popular colours were smoky grey, turquoise, yellow, and sea green. Clear glass was also used occasionally.

The emphasis was on decorative ornament and irregular, frosted, light-diffusing granular surfaces. Some of these ware were reminiscent of the designs of Marinot (see p.57). Alternatively, matt and polished surfaces were combined.

Decoration, either geometric or floral, tends to be freeform although it may be more formalized, as in the vase shown here (see right).

Most of the glass of the period is thick-walled and heavy in form. Being robust, it has generally survived well.

Marks

Most pieces are wheel-engraved with the words "Daum Nancy" and the insignia, the Cross of Lorraine (which was also used by other Nancy glassworks), but wares do not carry the names or initials of individual designers.

A large 1930s Daum vase of ovoid form, with collar neck. 12.5in (32cm) high E

Lamps

Second only to the vases, lamps were an important part of the factory's output during the Art Deco period. These etched glass lamps, with a frosted white ground and an acid-etched geometric design, are typical. Daum made glass lamps and also supplied glass shades for other lamps, most notably for the wrought-iron bases produced by Edgar Brandt (see pp.164–5).

Heavyweight lead glass was used for hanging and standard lamps. These items were mass-produced, but copied the labour-intensive hand-decorated work of such craftsmen as Décorchemont and Argy-Rousseau. From a distance they could be taken for *pâte-de-cristal*. Many of the lamps were mushroom-shaped and amber or amethyst with a mottled perimeter in contrasting colours. Surfaces were matt. They usually carry a wheel- or acid-cut signature.

The heavy forms of acid-etched glass produced by Lalique at this time are similar to those of Daum.

Examining Daum glass lamps

If possible, remove the metal mount and examine the neck of the base under a strong light – when the lamp is on the heat can cause the glass to crack. Internal cracks may not be readily apparent.

A Daum lamp. c.1925 18in (46cm) high D

A Daum table lamp, the clear glass matted in white. c.1925 16.5in (42cm) high D

Value point

The handmade pieces of the early Art Deco years fetch more than those from the industrial period of the later 1920s and 1930s.

Authenticity

Daum glass has been faked and so buyers should use a reputable source to purchase from. Wares are usually signed (see Marks, p.59).

Condition

The rims of Daum glass are usually gently rounded. A sharp edge might indicate that a chip has been removed. This practice might also be detected by examining the proportions.

Fakes

Some fakes have appeared on the market so far, although the acid-cut wares have been regarded by collectors as less important than the firm's Art Nouveau cameo wares. However, some lamps were copied by smaller French glassworks, using inferior moulded glass.

Colours

Daum used a few characteristic colours, the most common are:

- smoky grey
- green
- amethyst
- yellow/amber
- turquoise.

A Daum acid-etched chandelier, on a chipped ice ground. 1930 35in (89cm) high D

Gabriel Argy-Rousseau

An Argy-Rousseau "Lions" pâte-de-verre vase. 1926 8.75in (22cm) high C

1. Is the glass fairly small?
2. Is it *pâte-de-verre* (or more rarely, *pâte-de-cristal*)?
3. Is the decoration figural?
4. Is the glass relatively opaque?
5. Is the base moulded, but without visible mould lines?
6. Are rich colours employed?
7. Is the piece thin-walled and therefore relatively light for its size?
8.   Does the piece have a moulded signature?

Gabriel Argy-Rousseau (French, 1885–1953)

Initially a maker of false teeth, Argy-Rousseau first exhibited his *pâte-de-verre* in 1914, and from 1919 onwards made a series of enamelled scent bottles.

In 1921 he went into partnership with Gustave-Gaston Moser-Millot, who funded a workshop called Les Pâtes-de-verre d'Argy-Rousseau, where workers produced glassware designed by Argy-Rousseau and sold in Moser-Millot's shop. As well as vases and scent bottles, Argy-Rousseau made lamps, bowls, jars, jewellery, and perfume burners.

The glassworks were closed in 1931. Argy-Rousseau then worked on his own, making religious plaques (which are not popular with collectors) and angular vessels in streaked, jewel-like colours.

Recognition points

Pieces tend to be relatively small – most are under 9in (23cm) high. They are surprisingly light in weight.

Collecting

Les Pâtes-de-verre d'Argy-Rousseau produced glasswares in large quantities. The moulds were reusable but the pieces had to be coloured and finished by hand. Argy-Rousseau's later work is rarer. He is probably the most accomplished maker of *pâte-de-verre* and *pâte-de-cristal*. His Egyptian-inspired vases, and those depicting prowling wolves and lions, are considered the ultimate pieces among collectors, who pay large sums for them.

The use of figural decoration is characteristic, although he depicted a wide range of subjects including stylized flowers, fruit, birds, animals, and some rigidly geometric motifs.

Colours and finishes

Argy-Rousseau's pieces are usually richly coloured. He favoured white against tortoiseshell and mottled pinks against frosted ice. Green was also used.

Marks

All Argy-Rousseau's pieces are incised with his mark, which may appear as his initials, or "G. ARGY-ROUSSEAU" in capital letters, or in upper and lower case letters ("G. Argy-Rousseau").

An Argy-Rousseau "Masques" pâte-de-verre cabinet vase. c.1920 4in (10cm) high E

François-Emile Décorchemont

1. Is the item either *pâte-de-cristal* (partially translucent) or *pâte-de-verre* (dense and opaque)?
2. Is it heavy in form?
3. Are the colours bright – perhaps green or blue – and jewel-like?
4. Does the decoration contain either stylized subjects from nature or geometric images?
5. Is there an incise-cast signature?

François-Emile Décorchemont (French, 1880–1971)
Having first trained as a ceramist, Décorchemont began to experiment with *pâte-de-verre* glass, and then, in 1910, turned to *pâte-de-cristal*. From 1915 to 1926 he worked for Lalique, before setting up by himself at the Cristalleries de Saint-Rémy to make moulded glass. He became one of the most important exponents of *pâte-de-verre* (see p.49), but worked predominantly in *pâte-de-cristal*, concentrating on heavy forms, with an emphasis on internal colours and with the decoration deeply moulded (or engraved) on the exterior. By the 1930s he had turned away from art glass to concentrate on window panels.

A rare pâte-de-verre *"Conches" vase by Décorchemont. c.1925 5.5in (14cm) high C*

Recognition points
Décorchemont is known for the bright, jewelled colours that he developed using metallic oxides. He sought to produce uniform coloration, but he would often marble the colours to simulate semi-precious stones.

Marks
Pieces carry an incise-cast signature.

Amalric Walter

Amalric Walter (French, 1870–1959)
Like Décorchemont (see opposite), Walter began as a ceramist. In 1908 he joined the Daum workshops (see pp.58–61), where he made *pâte-de-verre* decorative wares, before setting up his own glassworks in 1919. He also produced a number of designs created by other Daum designers, such as the sculptor Henri Bergé, and local artists.

Walter's work is highly sculptural, as in this *pâte-de-verre* lizard (see right), dating from the 1920s. His style retained many elements of the Art Nouveau influence, and featured a variety of naturalistic motifs including small reptiles, frogs, insects, and goldfish. His pieces usually show a keen control of colour – for example, a salamander might be spotted for a more realistic effect.

Walter also made *pâte-de-verre* medallions, wall sconces, and decorative panels, but the mainstays of his output were the small useful or decorative pieces such as ashtrays, pin trays, brooches, and pendants.

Almaric Walter's *pâte-de-verre* is relatively heavy and opaque and usually includes more than one colour.

A 1920s Walter pâte-de-verre bowl. 6.75in (17cm) diam E

Marks
Pieces produced before 1914 are marked "DAUM NANCY" with the Cross of Lorraine. After 1919, Walter's work is signed "AW" or "A. WALTER NANCY"; the designer's signature is sometimes included as well. The mark or signature usually appears on the decorated surface at the side of the piece, rather than on the base, which is often ground to a smooth, flat finish. Fakes can be identified by their uninspiring colours and lack of depth.

Baccarat Crystal

A Baccarat "Ming Toy" figural perfume bottle, for Forest. c.1923 4.5in (11.5cm) high E

1. Is the piece well moulded?
2. Is the decoration either intaglio-moulded or enamelled?
3. Is the design restrained, with a Neo-classical or geometric influence?
4. Does the stopper incorporate a dropper?
5. Is the piece in clear glass?
6. Do the stopper and bottle belong together?
7. Is it signed?

Baccarat (French, 1764–present)

Baccarat designed bottles for a number of parfumiers, including d'Orsay, Jean Patou, Rimmel, Yardley, Elizabeth Arden, Coty, Roger & Gallet, Lentheric, and Guerlain. In the 1920s and 1930s, under the influence of the sculptor George Chevalier, the emphasis was on enamelling and geometric motifs and panel forms with sharp edges. Cut and moulded forms were also used, and there was often decorative staining.

Beware

Many of the stoppers incorporate an integral dropper; this is often damaged or missing. A danger is that a Baccarat stopper may have been matched to the wrong bottle: always examine the proportions and fit of any bottle and stopper.

Marks

The bottles are marked on the base with an acid-etched mark or a stencilled circle mark incorporating a central decanter and stopper flanked by a tumbler and wine glass. Baccarat is not known to have been faked, although the perfume bottles were copied.

Czech Bottles

In the 1920s and 1930s, the new demand in the scent trade for inexpensive perfume bottles was to a large extent satisfied by Czech glassworks: there were over 50 glassworks in Czechoslovakia during the 1920s and 1930s making mass-produced (rather than commissioned) glass perfume bottles.

Some of the glass can be relatively poorly moulded. However, the more inventive the design and the more they exemplify the Art Deco style, the more desirable (and costly) they are. Czech bottles are seldom marked, and as they are not highly individualistic, it is hard to distinguish between the various makers and factories.

Styles are often reminiscent of French bottles, although the Czech designers did not always copy French designs as has been suggested. The tinted and enamelled bottles resemble those of Baccarat.

Value point

Provided that they have survived intact, perfume bottles with atomizers usually command higher prices than those without.

A c.1920s Czechoslovakian perfume bottle. 6.25in (16cm) high G

Marius-Ernest Sabino

A Sabino bedside table lamp. c.1930 11in (28cm) high F

1. Is the glass moulded?
2. Is the piece opalescent throughout if tableware or a light fitting, or is the opalescence localized if a figure?
3. Are the mould lines evident?
4. If the piece is figural, are the female subjects stylized, with soft features and long legs?
5. If the glass is coloured is it blue, creamy white, or pale amber?

Marius-Ernest Sabino (French, 1878–1961)

From c.1923 until the closure of the glassworks in 1939, Sabino made a range of glass tablewares, lamps, and car mascots, many of them in a style that is strongly reminiscent of Lalique (see pp.50–5). However, the designs were intended for mass-production and as such were less expensive, and they remain so today.

Although competently executed and relatively attractive, most of his work is recognizably inferior when compared with that of Lalique. The quality of draftsmanship is often poor, and the mould lines may be very evident. However, certain pieces withstand comparison and are worth collecting, especially some of his figural wares and his ceiling lights.

Sabino has been accused of a lack of imagination in finding new motifs, instead borrowing images from other designers, especially Lalique, and rendering them in a relatively clumsy way. Nevertheless, even where using a familiar motif such as the dragonfly, Sabino occasionally achieved a pleasing synthesis of form and decoration with pieces that are delicate and well proportioned.

Note

Sabino is a minefield for collectors. Experience in observing and handling opalescent glass from the 1920s and 1930s may be of help in detecting a modern copy.

Signatures

Sabino signed his work in a variety of ways. The most usual form of signature was moulded. The engraved signature, which usually appears on pieces from the 1930s, takes the form of a large "S", with the rest of the name appearing in small script letters.

Later reproductions

Many of the moulds in which Sabino's designs were executed, were reused when the factory reopened in the 1960s. It can be difficult to tell which period a piece belongs to, as none of Sabino's work is dated or numbered. However, the more modern wares are likely to be less restrained in their use of opalescence than the earlier ones. Compare these with ones known to be from the 1920s or 1930s. Production ceased in 1975, although an American firm continued to make Sabino wares using the original moulds. These items carry a paper label that says "Sabino, made in France", but if this is missing the only way is to examine the piece for signs of natural wear.

Edmond Etling et Cie (French, active 1920s and 1930s)

Opalescent glass was also made by Etling. In addition to figures of female nudes, the firm made opalescent glass models of animals and ships, as well as a number of moulded vases, frequently of greyish glass with alternate polished and matt sections.

The body of this opalescent figurine of a woman and a dog (see below), c.1925, is cloaked in folds rendered in a characteristic pale bluish tint.

Etling also commissioned and retailed bronze and ivory statuettes by a number of leading designers.

An Etling "Femme avec Chien" opalescent glass figure. c.1925 7in (18cm) high G

69

Marcel Goupy

1. Is the decoration enamelled?
2. Is the form very simple?
3. Does the decoration show a balanced use of colour and an avoidance of harsh tones?
4. Is the rim finished with a fine enamel trim?
5. Is the glass relatively thick-walled and hand-blown?
6. Is the signature applied to a polished pontil mark on the base?

A Goupy enamelled glass vase, with stylized birds, designed c.1925 7.5in (19cm) high G

Marcel Goupy (French, 1886–1977)

Goupy was artistic director at La Maison Rouard from 1909 until 1954, and designed both forms and decoration. He concentrated on a range of small utilitarian enamelled glasswares, including drinking glasses, boxes, decanters, and vases. From the end of the 1920s some of his glasswares were engraved. He also created some designs for ceramics, occasionally to match glasswares, but also as independent pieces or sets, or for ceramics firms, such as Sèvres. Favoured motifs include nudes, landscapes, birds, flowers, and some mythological scenes. From c.1925,

in common with the work of other designers, motifs became somewhat more geometric.

Between 1919 and 1923 the enamelled decoration on many of his designs was executed by Auguste Heiligenstein.

Although he used bright colours, Goupy avoided the garishness that characterizes much glassware of the period, especially some Bohemian glass, which favoured the use of sharp contrasts. Art Deco items that are decorated with musicians or nightclub scenes tend to command a premium.

Recognition point

The glass base is an important feature of Goupy's glass and the decoration is sympathetic to the body – unlike other French glassware on which the enamel is so thick that it obscures the base.

Signatures

All the designs by Heiligenstein bear Goupy's signature in enamel but some items are unsigned.

Condition

Goupy's enamelled glasswares tend to have survived in good condition (unlike those of Ena Rottenberg, see below), as the enamels, which were evenly applied, are well fused with the glass.

Ena Rottenberg (Austrian, 1893–1962)

Rottenberg produced a distinctive type of enamelled glass. Wares are small – even vases are seldom taller than 12in (30.5cm). Light and shade are used to create a three-dimensional effect. The hand-blown glass is usually thin-walled, is of mixed quality, and often shows a pontil mark on the underside. The base is usually thick. Pieces are unsigned and do not carry the mark of the firm Loebmeyer, who executed many of the designs. Subjects are predominantly female, and are often semi-naked and depicted in a classical pose.

Jean Luce (French, 1895–1964)

Jean Luce designed enamel-decorated glasswares, mostly with floral or geometric motifs. Some designs were stylized. Like Goupy, he made matching tablewares and glasswares, including designs for the ocean liner SS *Normandie*.

Later work was experimental and abstract, and used a variety of techniques, including acid-etching and sand-blasting. Some pieces are reminiscent of the work of Marinot (see p.57), especially those with contrasting smooth and rough surfaces. His subtle decorations were usually rendered in a limited colour palette.

A Luce vase. c.1930
7.25in (18.5cm) high G

Orrefors Glassworks

An Orrefors jug, engraved with a female dancer, by Simon Gate. 1927 8.75in (22cm) high F

1. Does the decoration convey a sense of movement or fluidity?
2. Is the form inventive?
3. Are any women in the decoration stylized, with athletic postures?
4. Does the form complement the subject of the decoration – for example, are underwater scenes on rippled glass?
5. Is the design engraved or frosted, and possibly encased between layers of glass?
6. Is the glass clear, or with a faint blue tint, or a pale smoky effect?
7. Is the piece signed?

Orrefors (Swedish, 1898–present)

The factory mainly made utilitarian wares, but collectors look for innovative engraved or internally decorated wares. The inventive decoration includes pieces decorated on both sides to give a three-dimensional effect. Popular motifs are engraved nudes, Neo-classical scenes, and legends.

The firm is best known for its Graal wares, developed by Simon Gate in 1916 and refined during the 1920s. They were made using a cameo technique by which the design was etched onto the glass and then encased in a clear outer layer. Early Graal is often tinted; orange-brown was particularly popular. Designs by Edvard Hald are more up-to-the-minute than Gate's.

An Orrefors pressed glass vase, designed by Simon Gate. c.1930 6.25in (16cm) high H

Orrefors glass of the 1930s was heavier than it had been in the 1920s, and designs became bolder and more emphatic, with a greater degree of stylization. Vicke Lindstrand, who had a more Modernist approach than Gate, joined the firm in 1927/8. In the 1930s he developed "Ariel" glass, manipulating the glass to create unusual effects, for example, to suggest the undulating surface of water by trapping air bubbles between layers of clear glass and forming them into patterns.

Tints

Much Orrefors glass, especially that produced in the 1920s, is subtly tinted although on first inspection it appears clear. The tint can be discerned at the rim when the piece is turned on its edge.

Marks

Bases are usually engraved with "O.f.m" or "Orrefors" and with the name of the designer and engraver, and often with a year code and shape number as well.

Simon Gate (Swedish, 1883–1945)

Gate was the leading designer at Orrefors from 1917. His work is readily distinguished from that of the other engravers by the employment of deep surface engraving, Neo-classical style, and muscular stylized figures, more often women than men.

Steuben Glassworks

A Steuben engraved "Gazelle" bowl with stand, designed by Sidney Waugh. 1935 7in (18cm) high B

1. If the piece is engraved, is the engraving quite fine?
2. If a figural piece, are the figures highly stylized?
3. Is the crystal unusually pure and clear?
4. Is the form quite restrained?
5. Is the piece marked?

Steuben Glassworks (American, 1903–2011)

The company was founded by Frederick Carder (see below), and became a division of Corning in 1918. Before 1930 Carder designed many items himself. After 1930 the company employed a number of leading designers. From 1933 it produced only items of colourless pure crystal, with swelling fluid forms complemented by engraved designs. Most of the Art Deco work was produced by Sidney Waugh and Walter Dorwin Teague.

Marks

Steuben glass made between 1903 and 1932 is usually acid-stamped on the base with a fleur-de-lys and "Steuben" on a scroll. After 1932 the word "Steuben" or just "S" was engraved.

Sidney Waugh (American, 1904–63)

Waugh was Chief Associate Designer from 1933 until his death. In the 1930s he developed a range of crystalware inspired by traditional, mythological themes, such as the bowl opposite, which shows his use of stylized animals.

Walter Dorwin Teague (American, 1883–1960)

Teague (see p.171) is best known for his industrial designs. In c.1932 he was employed by Steuben to create a range of stemware.

A Steuben vase, with applied alabaster glass handles. c.1929 12in (30.5cm) high E

The influence of Scandinavian design is evident in much of Teague's and Waugh's work.

Frederick Carder (British, 1863–1963)

Until he left Steuben in 1930, Carder designed many of the firm's finest items himself. He developed a number of innovative techniques, including "Aurene" ware, a line of iridescent glass in various colours, particularly gold and blue, made between 1904 and 1933 in a variety of forms, including vases and candlesticks. Styles did not vary greatly and pieces are therefore difficult to date.

Other glass

A Jobling glass celery vase. 1934 7.75in (19.5cm) high H

Most inexpensive glass from the 1920s and 1930s is moulded and often geometric in form. Female nudes were the most popular motifs. Much of the work available uses debased Lalique designs; this is especially true of glass produced by the lesser French and Czech glassworks and also some manufacturers from North-East England. However, there has been interest in the cloud glass made in England by Davidson and in the "Chippendale" glass the firm produced from American designs. Some attempts

were made at producing British art glass by Gray-Stan, and also, from c.1922 by Monart in Perth, Scotland. Several Venetian glassworks at Murano, notably Venini and Salviati, made a number of figurines of dancing maidens, often in opaque white glass and supported on black hoop bases.

The North-East England company Jobling & Co. produced machine-made pressed glass in a similar style to that of Sabino (see p.68). In 1933 the firm introduced a range of art glass using French-inspired designs, including a limited number of opalescent wares. A high-gloss surface was typical, but the designs were not very successful, and the forms uninteresting.

A 1930s Royal Brierley cut glass vase, designed by Keith Murray. 12in (30.5cm) high F

At Royal Brierley, the designer, Keith Murray (see pp.106–7), introduced more modern decorative elements into the work of British factories that had been producing mainly fussy, opulent, brilliant-cut lead crystal glassware in Victorian patterns, which remained popular at the beginning of the century. His designs (see below left) were among the most striking and original glass made in Britain at the time.

Art Deco perfume atomizers often imitate designs by Lalique. The mechanisms are usually the same, although Lalique's mounts were all made by one manufacturer. The atomizer in this form was invented in the 1920s.

Many scent bottles were produced in France (with restrained designs) and Czechoslovakia (often with figural decoration and occasionally with outrageous forms and proportions, see p.67). The market has grown for the better ones: the main criteria are quality of execution and novelty. If bottles retain their packaging, and were made for quality perfumes, this adds to their value. Do not assume that any contents are the original perfume, as sometimes

A Czechoslovakian perfume atomizer. c.1930 5in (12.5cm) high H

bottles are filled with a coloured liquid for display purposes in stores or auction houses.

Many of the tablewares that survive from the period are Czech and are unmarked. They tend to imitate French designs: the decanter (see below) has a Baccarat feel (see p.66). The silver and black geometric enamel decoration was very popular in the 1920s and 1930s. The glasses are in good condition, with the enamel intact; it is rare to find a full set.

A 1930s Czechoslovakian art glass decanter set. Decanter 9in (23cm) high F

CERAMICS

Many of the ceramics from the 1920s and 1930s available on the market today consist of high-quality work by top designers. At the other end of the market there are many inexpensive items (see pp.126–7), which are good entry level. Tablewares predominate, and are usually sold as single pieces: it is not necessary to collect sets.

The most influential British potter of the period was Clarice Cliff (see pp.92–7), whose brightly coloured pieces were produced by the Newport Pottery in Staffordshire. Many of these wares are hybrids of traditional shapes, forms, and techniques, and more Modernist decorative elements. Cliff had many imitators, and an enormous quantity of Clarice Cliff lookalikes were produced. Other major designers include Susie Cooper (see pp.98–101) and manufacturers such as Burleigh and Myott (see pp.126–7), which produced wares in original shapes. However, the output of most British potteries during this period, even those who did try to modernize part of their range, remained essentially traditional.

This period saw a growing use of glaze effects. Lustre wares were made famous by Wedgwood (see pp.102–5), and were emulated by a number of other firms,

including C. T. Maling in Newcastle. The Lancastrian Pottery's innovative decorative technique for its Lapis ware used pigment and glaze fused into the body; however, it continued to use traditional forms. By contrast, Shelley (see pp.108–9) and Royal Doulton (see pp.112–13) were known for their stark white bone china.

There was a growing market for ornaments, many retailed through seaside shops. Small animal figurines by SylvaC and others found a ready market. Painted chalk figures, especially of the variety showing damsels being walked by borzois, were also popular, but are not regarded as important today. Those that do survive tend to be in poor condition, as chalk blisters in strong sunlight and fractures easily. Cheap Czech Art Deco figurines and glassware (see p.77) were imported into Britain during this period: most of these, too, are not worth collecting, as they look mass-produced and are often badly made.

In Italy, Gio Ponti produced figures similar to the stylish porcelain and earthenware pieces by the Lenci factory in Turin (see pp.116–19), as well as tasteful wares for Ginori, in which design and decoration complement each other.

A Clarice Cliff "Chahar" wall mask. c.1930 11in (28cm) high F

In Germany, Rosenthal (see p.123) and several other bone china and porcelain manufacturers worked in a clean, classical style, especially in their tablewares. In Vienna, Goebel and Hutschenreuther made figurines. Earthenware and figures were produced by Katzhütte.

In Austria, Goldscheider (see pp.120–2) made figures, wall masks, and large earthenware sculptures as well as plaster and ceramic versions of the bronzes of Lorenzl, Zach, and other major sculptors, which were exported to the United States.

In France, Limoges, which employed a number of top designers, continued to be the main centre for mass-produced ceramics, but even traditional forms provided the mainstay of production. The firms of Robj and Argilor popularized the novelty night-light, which they produced in porcelain, often using Middle Eastern figures such as harem girls and turbaned servants.

Some of the most "modern"-looking pieces produced during this period come from Scandinavia. Interesting animal sculptures by Knud Khyn use stoneware covered with heavy celadon and orange-green glazes.

American ceramics in the Art Deco style are either pieces designed by prominent artists in progressive styles and made to high technical and artistic standards, or more readily available French-inspired or "streamline" wares, made for mass consumption during the 1930s. Among the most heavily collected of this second type are the Fiesta wares and other products of the Homer Laughlin China Company, most of which use bright monochrome glazes. Geometrically stylized wares by the Rookwood Pottery bear impressed marks, and are mostly finished with matt monochrome glazes. Similar glazes and styles are found on the later products of the Fulper and Weller potteries, most of which bear clear printed marks. A line of highly geometric designed vases with matt, polychrome glazes was sold from c.1928 by the Roseville Pottery in Ohio, under the trademark Futura. It is a much more interesting design than Roseville's earlier wares. Frank Ferrell was Roseville's artistic director from 1917.

In 1927 the Cowan Pottery added the Cowan Pottery Studio Inc., which produced impressive and advanced designs by designers and highly collectable "studio" lines. Its output included the highly stylized "Jazz" punchbowl (see pp.124–5).

Many wares are marked. Collectors should familiarize themselves with the marks and signatures used during the period by consulting *Miller's Antiques Marks* by Judith Miller.

A Goldscheider figure of a lady, by Josef Lorenzl. c.1930 15.25in (39cm) high E

René Buthaud

A 1920s Buthaud vase, with incised Nubian nudes and palm fronds. 24.25in (61.5cm) high D

1. Is the decoration geometric or figural (perhaps depicting a Neo-classical or African subject), and linear, with stylized features?
2. Is the form earthenware rather than porcelain?
3. Do any female figures have firm, painted outlines?
4. Does the palette show a preference for blue-grey and/or iron red?
5. Is the ground stone or cream colour?
6. Is the form relatively conventional?

René Buthaud (French, 1886–1986)

Buthaud trained as a silver decorator before studying art in Paris. As well as pottery, he also executed graphics, watercolours, and stained-glass window designs. Some of his posters have the same idealized females that appear on his ceramics. The influence of other painters, especially Jean Dupas (see pp.200–1), is evident in his work. Other pieces had Neo-classical imagery.

Buthaud first worked in ceramics after the First World War, and his vases were first exhibited in 1920. His faïence vases had hand-painted figural decoration, often with brown or green outlines.

His ceramics, predominantly vases of simple form, were usually either painted, crackle-glazed, or sgraffito. The earthenware vase (see left) from the 1920s, which is incised with highly stylized nudes, is typical of his sgraffito work in its dark, chocolatey-brown tones against a paler earthenware body. The figural decoration on sgraffito wares often depicts African subjects.

Sgraffito

Buthaud was one of the principal exponents of sgraffito, or carved away decoration – the word is Italian for "scratched", and refers to the technique by which a pottery body is dipped in a separate slip of another colour, through which the decoration is then carved.

Availability

Buthaud was not prolific and prices tend to be high. Geometric designs usually have a brown palette. Buthaud was among the artists who incorporated African motifs into their work following the success of the Revue Nègre.

Crackle-glazed earthenware vases bear a painted "R. Buthaud", or incised or painted monogram, "RB".

Emile Lenoble (French, 1876–1939)

Lenoble was another French studio potter who used the sgraffito technique on stoneware. Glazes were matt or textured rather than polished. Motifs were geometric or floral and stylized.

A Lenoble art pottery vase. c.1930
9.5in (24cm) high F

Sèvres

A Sèvres porcelain vase, designed by Anne-Marie Fontaine. 1927 8.25in (21cm) high F

1. Is the piece of particularly high quality?
2. Is the form relatively conventional, with any innovative elements in the piece being provided by the decoration?
3. Is the surface heightened in some way, perhaps with gilt or heavy pigment?
4. Is the piece signed?

Sèvres (French, 1750–present)

From 1920 Sèvres was under the direction of Georges LeChevallier-Chévignard. He employed a number of top designers, including some who traditionally worked in other media. The factory's reputation was such that he was able to call upon the top designers of the day.

Decoration and glazes

The output of the factory in the Art Deco period tended to rely on elaborate decoration rather than innovative shapes. The quality of the wares was exceptionally high.

- Egyptian motifs and geometric decoration were often used.
- Glazes were frequently heightened with gilt decoration.

Designers and decorators

Leading designers of the era included Henri Rapin and Jacques-Emile Ruhlmann (see pp.14–17).

- Some inventive designs and slightly unconventional forms represented a departure for Sèvres from its usual straightforward, commercially safe shapes adapted from 18thC designs for dinner and tea wares.
- There is usually a harmony between

form and decoration, such as a large expanse of ivory porcelain juxtaposed with a busy design.

- Other designers and decorators include: Robert Bonfils, Emile Decoeur, Jean Dupas, Anne-Marie Fontaine, Suzanne Lalique, François Pompon, and Taxile Doat. Their marks usually appear on the footrim.

Marks

Sèvres wares were signed between 1738 and 1954, but signatures should be regarded with caution. At least 80% of 18thC and 19thC porcelain with the Sèvres mark was not made at the factory – many factories producing wares at the same time freely copied the mark. However, in the late 19thC a new system was introduced at Sèvres that showed the letter "S" with the date underneath, contained in a triangle. This mark was rarely copied and is seldom faked.

Note

It is particularly difficult to provide an extensive checklist for Sèvres wares in the Art Deco period as the designs are so individual and were executed by a number of designers given creative freedom.

A Sèvres box and cover.
c.1925 6.5in (16.5cm) diam F

Boch Frères

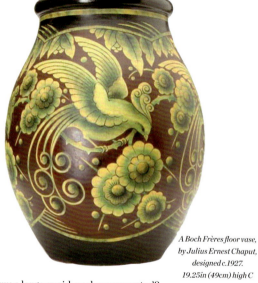

A Boch Frères floor vase,
by Julius Ernest Chaput,
designed c.1927.
19.25in (49cm) high C

1. Is the form a large ovoid, perhaps mounted?
2. Are the surface enamels thickly applied?
3. Have bold primary colours been used?
4. Is the decoration applied over the glaze?
5. If the reserve colour is pale, is it ivory rather than white?
6. Is there a crackle, or craquelure, effect under a thick glaze?
7. Is there a signature?

Boch Frères (1767–present)

The Belgian firm Boch Frères was founded in 1767 at Sept Fontaines in the Saarland (Germany), but by the mid-19thC, following a split, part of the firm established its manufactory, Boch Frères, Keramis, in Belgium. It produced mainly earthenware vases, some tablewares, and candlesticks. Boch Frères wares of the mid-1920s–40s represent the most important Belgian contribution to Art Deco.

- Some stonewares were also produced.
- Both the earthenware and the stoneware produced by the firm in this period are white-bodied.

Other crackle wares

The wares produced by Boch Frères are similar in treatment to Czech Amphora wares. These are also heavily enamelled with incised, deeply moulded outlines. Other firms producing wares with crackled glazes beneath painted or enamelled decoration were the French firm Longwy, for Primavera (see pp. 90–1), and the English pottery, Poole (see pp.110–11), which used a more subtle crackle effect.

Charles Catteau (French/Belgian, 1880–1966)

Vases designed by Catteau (see right, above right, and pp.88–9) were often monumental in size (some were

A Boch Frères vase, by Charles Catteau. 1924
14in (35.5cm) high E

A Boch Frères vase, by Charles Catteau. 1924
14in (35.5cm) high G

A Boch Frères vase, decorated with stylized flying pelicans. 1925 13.75in (35cm) high F

- Incised stylized flowers pendant from the rim are often used.
- Favourite colours were deep green, blue, black, and brown.
- Forms could be of a simple ovoid shape, with little or no base and a narrow rim.
- Later designs were more geometrically elaborate – for example, the ovoid form might be extended at the base.

48in/122cm high) and decorated with thickly applied enamel motifs, which stand out in relief from the background. This is often of a thickly glazed ivory with a craquelure effect.

Catteau is often regarded as one of the most versatile ceramic artists of his generation. He advanced the forms and decoration of ceramics, creating an original, new, and decorative genre.

- The choice of an animal in a naturalized setting is typical.
- Other designs are linear or zigzag, with stylized animals – perhaps penguins or leaping gazelles.

A Boch Frères vase, "Bouquet Stylisé", by Charles Catteau. c.1927 12.5in (32cm) high E

A Boch Frères vase, decorated in cuerda seca *with stylized penguins. 1927 14.5in (37cm) high D*

A. W. Finch

Along with the leading Keramis designer in the Art Deco period, Charles Catteau (see pp.87–8), an early contribution was made by the English artist Arthur Finch, who worked for Boch Frères as a decorator until 1930. His vases employ the large, swollen design typical of the factory, but he used a red background in slip and glazed ochre to the dark green and blue motifs.

Marks

Keramis wares bear a number of marks.
- Some pieces are stamped "KERAMIS MADE IN BELGIUM" and carry a painted design number.

Others may be stamped "BOCH FES LA LOUVIERE MADE IN BELGIUM FABRICATION BELGE". These may also have a style and pattern number.
- Alternatively, they may bear a painted "B.F.K" and a style number.
- Some pieces also bear the name of the designer, such as an inscribed "Keramis" with the painted mark "Ch. Catteau D.1082 B.F.K.".

A Boch Frères Keramis vase, designed by Charles Catteau. 1931 12in (30.5cm) high G

Primavera

A Primavera stoneware vase, painted with a horse and an antelope. c.1930 12.75in (32.5cm) high F

1. Is the item pottery?
2. If it is an animal, is it devoid of colour, relying instead on a monochrome glaze, perhaps crackled?
3. Is the decoration stylized?
4. Are the colours subtly blended, with muted glazes?
5. Is the shape avant-garde?
6. Does it have an incise-moulded signature?

Primavera (French, 1920s and 1930s)

Primavera was the design studio of the Parisian department store Au Printemps and was one of the leading salons of the Art Deco period. The firm produced a range of ceramic wares, including figures and simple monochrome animal studies.

- Forms are characteristically relatively simple but original, with a sculptural quality.
- The most desirable Primavera wares are the handmade artist-decorated ones, although those made in a mould are also collectable.

Primavera figures are usually very stylized, and often convey a strong sense of movement. The subjects may be unusual in not having the lithe figures commonly associated with Art Deco women. In particular, the legs may be somewhat thick and unshapely.

Glazes

Primavera earthenware tends to have a reddish tone, often with evidence of some gentle crazing, usually apparent from the inside. Many of those produced for Primavera were made by the Longwy factory and bear that name.

Condition

The value of a piece is inevitably affected by damage. However, as items that are bought as much for their academic or scarcity value as for their decorative value, the fall in price is not great.

Marks

Handmade Primavera wares are invariably signed on the base, usually by the potter/modeller and the decorator, and in addition always carry the Primavera mark. Signatures are either hand-painted or are impressed in block capitals. Moulded wares carry an incise-moulded signature.

Well-known decorators and designers who worked for the design studio include Claude Levy, Colette Gueden, the wife of the director, Charlotte Chaucet-Guillere, Jean Jacques Adnet, René Buthaud (see pp.82–3), Marcel Renard, Madeleine Saugez, and Léon Zack.

A Primavera vessel, with panels of nude women. c.1930 16.5in (42cm) high F

Clarice Cliff

A Clarice Cliff Bizarre Stamford "Orange Roof Cottage" teapot and cover. c.1930 5in (12.5cm) high F

1. Are motifs bold and decisive?
2. Are colours bright, almost garish?
3. Are landscapes highly stylized?
4. Is the piece hand-painted?
5. Are enamels laid on thickly, so that brush strokes are visible?
6. Is the shape inventive and almost futuristic?
7. Is there any black outline or banding, either around motifs or rims?
8. Is there a mark on the base?

Clarice Cliff (British, 1899–1972)

Clarice Cliff dominated the British pottery scene during the late 1920s and 1930s. She joined A. J. Wilkinson's Royal Staffordshire Pottery in Burslem in 1916, where she learned all aspects of pottery-making including the modelling and firing of wares. In 1927 the firm recognized Cliff's talent and enthusiasm and set her up in a studio in their nearby Newport Pottery with a team of paintresses. The first pieces were very successful and she became a household name, continuing to produce a wide range of wares until the outbreak of the Second World War.

Wares

Tablewares dominate the range, among them tea sets, trays, jugs, bowls, baskets, and so on. Cliff also designed book ends, candlesticks, figurines, and masks. A distinctive and very extensive range of shapes and patterns were used. Many forms are highly innovative – exemplified by the cone-shaped sugar sifter (see p.94), beehive honey pot, and futuristic bowl (see right) – but Cliff also produced more traditional wares that represented an economically safe compromise. Her first successful range, Bizarre Ware, was launched in 1928. Other ranges followed soon after, with patterns gradually becoming more elaborate, although Cliff took care to ensure that each design was fully applicable to a full range of shapes and sizes.

Lines were exclusive and sold in many top department stores. As a result, there were many cheaper imitations on the market, which can still be found today.

Identification

The pottery was produced by Wilkinsons at its Newport works in Stoke-on-Trent. The company's pattern books and contemporary advertisements can be used to identify patterns. Sometimes different names were used for the different colours in which patterns appeared.

Glazes

The body of pieces is earthenware, covered in a distinctive "honey glaze", a warm yellow-tinted glaze that gives

A Clarice Cliff Bizarre bowl, with the "Applique Lucerne" pattern. c.1931 6in (15.5cm) diam F

an ivory colour. Glazing is not rigidly controlled. Enamels are usually laid on relatively thickly so that the brush strokes are visible.

Condition

Check condition carefully. Restoration is not always easy to detect. Look particularly at spouts and handles, and run a finger around rims and bases to check for chipping or repainting. Look out for any slight variation in the colour where the pattern may have been touched up.

Collecting

Cliff pieces are usually collected by pattern or object, rather than in sets. Look for a good balance of form and pattern. "Crocus", the earliest floral design, is the least collectable range because it was so popular at the time and therefore produced in large quantities. Similarly, the more traditional shapes are less desirable. Rare shapes, usually those with unusual rims or flanges caused by warping in the kiln, or those made in several sections joined together, are also desirable. Collectors like the strong geometric forms; floral moulded pieces tend to ignored, as do the flower vases in water lily form. The rarest range is Inspiration (see p.97), followed by others that use experimental techniques. Cliff's

A Clarice Cliff Bizarre "Cornwall" sugar sifter. c.1933 5.5in (14cm) high G

extensive range included many small objects, providing an opportunity for the collector of miniatures or for those with limited space or budget.

Shapes and themes

Cliff designed all her own wares, which were then hand-painted, sometimes by a number of people in production-line fashion. The various ranges are named, as are some glaze techniques.

• Early geometric patterns are regular

in design and employ wide bands of colour.

- Later patterns are more abstract and use finer banding, sometimes to provide a textured background to floral or landscape motifs. Decoration is sometimes, but not always, outlined in black.
- Many wares depict landscapes; these have a lot in common with the work of illustrators and stained-glass artists of the period. Many show cottages (especially with a red roof) in country gardens, or a house at the side of a hill, as in the teapot on p.92.
- Trees are often drawn with long, spindly trunks surmounted by clouds of foliage.

A Clarice Cliff "Circus" plate, designed by Dame Laura Knight. c.1934 9in (23cm) diam H

Circus series

This plate (see above), one of a set, was designed c.1934 by Laura Knight as part of her now very collectable Circus series for Clarice Cliff (although the series was not a great commercial success in the 1930s). The borders and faces are printed, while the rest is hand-painted in stencil, then gilded.

Other leading Cliff designers included Dod Proctor and Graham Sutherland, who designed a dinner service decorated with a lively horse motif. Frank Brangwyn designed large circular plaques colourfully decorated with figural subjects (taken from panels originally intended to be hung in the Palace of Westminster).

Fakes

Genuine Cliff can usually be distinguished from the many reproductions and fakes on the market. The standard of painting on the fakes is usually poor and the colour enamels washed out. The honey glaze is often murky, and unevenly applied. Some are relatively competent but lack the definition of genuine pieces. Also, handles may be a little thin, and unglazed footrims narrow and irregular. Many have a tendency towards pronounced ribbing.

Fakes can also be identified by the marks. On genuine pieces the mark is

A Clarice Cliff "Floreat" pattern meiping vase. 1929–30 12in (30.5cm) high E

A fake Clarice Cliff of the "Applique Caravan" pattern. c.1930 12in (30.5cm) high Under £10

usually smooth. A crackle effect may be cause for suspicion (although a few genuine pieces have appeared with such crazing).

- On flatware, three circles or stilt marks around the signature where the pot stood in the kiln are a sign of authenticity.
- There are also some genuine reproductions, but these are clearly dated.

Figures and novelty wares

"Age of Jazz" figures, such as those showing dancing couples, are much sought after. These have a three-dimensional effect but are in fact

freestanding plaques. Not all novelty items are highly collectable – for example, Cliff toby jugs have never been in strong demand.

Masks

The series of masks (see p.79), which includes wall pockets and some very desirable wall masks, is very collectable, geometric types being the most desirable. Cliff designed some of these pieces herself; others bear the incise-cast initials of the designer. The best examples are relatively well modelled, with a lot of facial creasing. Moulded floral garlands are popular: other Cliff masks tended to feature various types of floral headdresses.

In Cliff masks the subject is shown face-on; on masks by rival firms they tend to be in profile.

Inspiration series

Wares decorated with the Inspiration design (see below) and executed in the characteristic blue and lilac colours are particularly sought after. Look for a hand-painted signature on the base.

Marks

Most but not all pieces are marked. A variety of different marks was used. Pieces often carry impressed dates, although these may indicate the date of production rather than that of design or decoration. The pattern name was often given alongside the Clarice Cliff signature. Pattern names and signatures were initially handwritten; later they were stamped and eventually, they were lithographed.

Pieces also carry the factory name, which was printed. Marked fakes exist but can usually be identified as such (see pp.95–6).

• Hand-painted signatures and marks were phased out by c.1931.

A Clarice Cliff Inspiration "Knight Errant" charger. c.1930 18in (46cm) diam E

Susie Cooper

A Gray's Pottery "Moon and Mountain" coffee set, designed by Cooper.
c.1930 coffee pot 7.75in (19.5cm) high E

1. Is the form relatively traditional, possibly rounded, with innovation perhaps confined to any lid or handle?

2. If a tea set, is it in autumnal shades?

3. Is the piece earthenware?

4. Does the decoration have any floral motifs, thick bands of bright colours, or a spotted design?

5. Is the decoration precisely executed, with great attention to detail, and an element of understatement?

6. Does the piece have a robust feel?

7. Is it signed? (But see Marks, p.101)

Susie Cooper (British, 1902–95)

Susie Cooper worked for A. E. Gray, c.1925–30, decorating a variety of wares in floral, abstract, or, more rarely, geometric designs. Some of her early work for Gray has lustre trims or finishes in a variety of colours. Initially, she followed established patterns, but soon was allowed to design her own. During this period Cooper produced wares with solid bands of colours with as many as five or six colours on one piece. Unlike on similar wares by Clarice Cliff (see pp.92–7), these thick bands of colour were not isolated, but have a more random, naïve feel. Cooper often used overall decoration on her designs. Geometric and floral motifs were sometimes combined on one piece. She also designed some nursery wares for Gray.

Susie Cooper Pottery (British, 1931–79)

From 1930 Cooper designed and produced her own wares, buying blanks (undecorated earthenware bases) from other manufacturers. In 1931 she set up her own pottery, the Susie Cooper Pottery, in Burslem, Staffordshire. Designs were generally rather understated, certainly when compared to those of Clarice Cliff (see pp.92–7). A few had sgraffito decoration, but most were hand-painted.

A Cooper geometric coffee pot. c.1928
8in (20.5cm) high H

A Cooper "Cubist" jug. 1929
4.75in (12cm) high H

From the mid-30s some designs were lithographed or transfer-printed, but they nevertheless retained a hand-finished feel. Colours became more subtle in this period, autumnal shades were particularly preferred. The pottery produced a range of wares, in particular vases, jugs, and tea and dinner sets.

Clean, traditional designs were tempered with innovation – for example, tureens often had a self-supporting lid that could be turned upside down and used as a serving dish.

Decorative techniques

Susie Cooper used a variety of techniques, including under- and overglazed decoration, and experimented with new methods, such as sgraffito, crayons, and tube-lining.

Incised stonewares

A series of incised stonewares was produced in the 1930s. Flowers and feathered leaves were preferred, as well as patterns with bright dots, dashes, and even exclamation marks. Most tea sets were decorated in autumnal russet and greens.

A Susie Cooper biscuit barrel. c.1932 5.5in (14cm) diam H

Collecting

The most collectable wares are those made before 1939. After the Second World War, bone china replaced earthenware as her favoured material. This is lighter in weight than earthenware and less

A Susie Cooper stoneware vase, inscribed with flowers. c.1938 10in (25.5cm) high H

100

robust in appearance. Collectors will find a catalogue of her wares very helpful in distinguishing between pre- and post-war designs, especially as many of the designs from the 1920s and 1930s have been reproduced since the Second World War.

Shapes and forms

Most Susie Cooper wares have shape and pattern names and numbers. Shapes used from the 1930s include The Kestrel (introduced 1932), Curlew (1932), Wren (1934), Jay (1935), Falcon (1937), and Spiral (1938). The "Dresden Spray" pattern was first used c.1935 and was one of her most popular. Others from the period include "Tadpoles", "Scarlet runner beans", "Nosegay", "Polka dots', and "Cromer".

Patterns were not usually confined to a specific shape but might appear on any number of forms.

Marks

Some, but not all, of the Gray wares decorated

A Susie Cooper "Skier" mug. 1933–4 3.75in (9.5cm) high H

by Cooper have a printed backstamp and her initials SV (for Vera) C or SC. Her designs were still used after she left the firm, although not always on the original shapes: the pattern numbers during Cooper's period at Gray are those between the late 2000s and the mid-8000s. Numbers that are not within these figures cannot be Susie Cooper designs.

A Susie Cooper "Angel Fish" table centre. 1936 10.75in (27.5cm) high F

Josiah Wedgwood & Sons

A Wedgwood sculpture, by John Skeaping. 1927 7in (18cm) high H

1. Is the piece an animal or bird?
2. If an animal, is it in a passive stance?
3. Does the piece have a reflective matt or semi-matt glaze in cream, celadon green moonstone, or black basalt?
4. If a figure, is the area underneath it filled in, and possibly decorated – for example, with formalized shrubbery?
5. Is the "J. Skeaping" mark incise-cast into the side of the piece, together with the impressed Wedgwood mark?

Josiah Wedgwood & Sons (British, 1759–present)

During the Art Deco period Wedgwood produced traditional and avant-garde designs. Apart from the work of Keith Murray (see pp.106–7), the most significant contribution to Wedgwood Art Deco design was the work of John Skeaping. Other Wedgwood designers of the period were: Eric Ravilious (see p.104), Norman Wilson (who experimented with glaze effects), Victor Skellern, Millicent Taplin, Alfred and Louise Powell (best known for lustre decoration), Anna Katrina Zinkeisen, and Erling B. Olsen.

John Skeaping (British, 1901–80)

Skeaping was employed as a designer by Wedgwood from 1926. He specialized in animal sculptures, and also made some birds, and his work influenced many lesser potters of the period. Of the 14 designs he created for Wedgwood, ten were in production through the 1930s. They were somewhat reminiscent of the work of the Swiss sculptor Edouard Marcel Sandoz (see pp.126 and 157).

Animals were usually produced first in basalt and then in a variety of colours and glazes – for example, the seal is often found in tan or celadon green.

Note

A number of Skeaping pieces have fitted wooden stands. If the object is a very tight fit the stand should be professionally removed, because the figures are prone to cracking as the wood tightens with age.

Other ceramic animals

With the notable exception of a bull designed by Arnold Machin printed with zodiac signs by Eric Ravilious, most Wedgwood animals of this period are by Skeaping. Similar wares were retailed by Primavera (see pp.90–1). Royal Lancastrian also produced animal figures (including bears, sea lions, and

A Wedgwood nursery ware "Alphabet" mug, by Ravilious. 1937 3.25in (8cm) high G

a gazelle). The Staffordshire Shaw & Copestake factory produced the very popular SylvaC range of rabbits and other novelty figures.

Eric Ravilious (British, 1903–42)

The attractive utility wares designed by Eric Ravilious for Wedgwood during the late 1930s are currently very popular with collectors. Prices have risen accordingly and even damaged items are collectable, although they fetch around half the price of perfect pieces.

- Ravilious designed his "Alphabet" nursery ware (see p.103) in 1937; the decoration was transfer-printed, usually in straightforward bands.

Pastel colours were used; pink, yellow and grey predominate. The shapes used for the range tended to be those used for the firm's standard current tableware.

- Other currently sought-after Ravilious designs are the boat-race chalice, a zodiac series, and a lemonade set decorated with garden implements. The pieces are still quite widely available and include whole dinner services.
- Most Ravilious designs were not executed in any quantities until the 1950s.
- Some of his designs were reissued in 1987 in response to an increase

A Wedgwood Fairyland lustre "Woodland Elves VIII – Boxing Match". c.1918 10.5in (26.5cm) diam F

in public demand. These pieces lack the characteristic signs of wear found on the originals.

Wedgwood lustre wares

During the 1920s and 1930s Wedgwood produced a range of lustre wares, including Chinese and Butterfly lustre, and the Fairyland series designed by Daisy Makeig-Jones, which is the most popular and expensive type.

- The imagery of pixies and goblins on Fairyland lustre is not usually associated with the Art Deco period and in fact harks back more to the fairytale world of c.1900, but the shapes and bright colours of these wares were considered to be comparatively "modern" and this made them popular with the public in the 1920s and 1930s.
- Some of the rarer examples of Daisy Makeig-Jones's work, such as rectangular plaques, bear her signature, usually in gilt, and often hidden among the decoration.
- Wedgwood Fairyland wares are identified by the letter Z and a pattern number on the base.
- Wedgwood's lustre wares were emulated by Carlton (see pp.114–15).

Wedgwood marks

In the 1920s and 1930s the impressed mark "Wedgwood, made in England"

A Wedgwood Fairyland lustre "Firbolg" malfrey pot. c.1920 9.5in (24cm) diam D

was used. The printed Portland vase mark on bone china dates from 1878 and continued to be used, in a slightly different form, in the 1920s and 1930s. After the 1940s the Barlaston mark was introduced on creamwares.

- Ravilious wares are signed in a small rectangular panel "designed by Eric Ravilious" and carry an imprinted Wedgwood mark.

Keith Murray

A Wedgwood matt green "Bombe" vase, designed by Keith Murray. 1930 6in (15.5cm) high H

1. Has the piece a simple geometric form?
2. Is any decoration integral to the form, rather than applied to the surface?
3. Is the glaze semi-matt?
4. Is the body earthenware?
5. Is it ribbed?
6. Is the piece signed with Murray's full script signature?

Keith Murray (New Zealander/British, 1892–1981)

Murray spent most of his working life in England. His background as an architect is evident in the architectural, Modernist ceramic wares he produced in the 1930s and 1940s. From the late 1930s he also made glass for the Staffordshire firm of Stevens & Williams (see pp.76–7) and was one of the few designers in England to promote Modernist principles in his designs.

Murray's work is recognizable for its simple geometric forms and lack of surface embellishment. He also produced inkstands, candlesticks, and litho-printed commemorative wares celebrating George VI. His slip-wares were introduced after 1936 and produced until the mid-1950s.

Authenticity

Murray's work, especially his vases and bowls, is much reproduced today.

A Wedgwood matt blue vase, shape number 3820, designed 1933. 7in (18cm) high F

However, these modern wares are not intended to deceive and they do not bear Murray's signature. The first rule in buying Murray is: if it's not marked, it's not Murray. Fakes deliberately intended to deceive have not so far appeared.

Glazes

Murray used a distinct range of glazes; these were matt, semi-matt, or celadon satin. Some have names – the ivory-white is known as "moonstone". Others include matt blue and matt grey.

• Some 1930s glazes continued to be produced after 1940, including green, moonstone, and straw.
• Post-1945 wares tend to have a crazed surface.

Tableware and patterns

From 1933 Murray designed tablewares and other functional but ornamental items for Wedgwood, as well as patterns for tableware. These included "Lotus", "Weeping Willow" (or "Green Tree"), "Iris", "Pink Flower", and "Pink and Red Flower", and the border pattern "Radio".

Signatures

A script signature appears on pre-war items. Those made after 1941 usually use the initials "KM" and the Barlaston mark. Murray's black basalt wares, the rarest of all his products, are signed in red on the base.

Shelley

*A Shelley Vogue tea service, decorated with the "Turkish Blue Blocks"
pattern. c.1930 G*

1. Do rims have silver lustre or coloured banding?
2. Are wares with geometric designs of good-quality bone china?
3. Do handles have innovative forms?
4. Is use made of the underlying ground in all-over decoration?
5. Is the design hand-painted in enamels with a transfer-printed
    outline?
6. Do the motifs include trees, flowers, and the sun?
7. Is the piece signed?

Shelley (British, 1872–1966)

The factory, originally known as Wileman & Co., and later trading under the name Foley, changed its name to Shelley in 1925, although the Shelley stamp had been used as early as 1910. During the 1920s and 1930s the firm tempered the more avant-garde lines with commercially safe classic shapes and designs. A large number of tea and dinner sets were made; complete sets are at a premium, especially those designed by Mabel Lucie Attwell. No fakes are known, although there are many contemporary lookalikes.

Decoration

Striking colour combinations include yellow and black, and mauve and green. Wares in jade green combined with a silver lustre trim are especially desirable. Colours became progressively more subdued and florals less stylized during the 1930s.

Collecting

Not all Shelley wares are sought after by collectors, but those from the Art Deco period are very desirable, in particular the shape named Eve, which combines an innovative design with practicality or fitness for purpose. The most successful designs are simple. Some of the more innovative ones proved impracticable – for example, Vogue and Mode had solid handles that were difficult to use, and these were not in production for very long.

Marks

All genuine Shelley wares are marked. A script signature inside a cartouche is the most common. Anything marked "Fine Bone China" is post-1945. Pattern numbers progressed from around 11,000 in the mid-1920s to around 13,000 in 1939. The serial number for seconds begins with a 2.

Nursery wares

This highly successful area for Shelley used the talents of two illustrators, Mabel Lucie Attwell, who joined the firm in 1926, and Hilda Cowham, who was taken on in 1928. They designed a range of children's wares, with unusual shapes, including a toadstool teapot (see below) and story-book-type illustrations. In the 1930s Attwell also designed an animal tea set and figurines of fairies. Nursery wares are still popular today.

A Shelley "Boo Boo" tea set by Mabel Lucie Attwell. c.1926 Milk jug 6.5in (16.5cm) high G

Poole Pottery

A Poole Pottery "Leaping Deer" pattern vase, designed by Truda Carter. 1934–7 8.25in (21cm) high F

1. Does the piece use a distinctive palette, perhaps with blue as the dominant colour?
2. Is the decoration stylized, possibly with floral motifs?
3. Does the piece have a semi-matt glaze?
4. Is the body red clay with an overlying grey-white glaze?
5. Is there an impressed Carter-Stabler-Adams mark and a painter's signature or mark?

Carter, Stabler and Adams (British, 1873–present)

This firm, which operated from the Poole Pottery in Dorset, was established as Carter and Co. In 1921 it expanded and took the combined surnames of its partners Charles Carter, Harold and Phoebe Stabler, and John Adams.

Although it was not known by this name until 1963, the firm's early wares are usually called Poole.

Ranges

Pieces are collected by design rather than by artist. Collectable ranges from the 1930s include:

- 1933 Studland, a plain body with elaborate and angular handles, in dark green or blue, or painted with modern leaves and flowers.
- c.1933 Picotee, rounded shapes, and Everest, ribbed, with solid diamond-shaped handles.
- 1936 Streamline, simplified traditional shapes, with two-colour glazes in subdued autumnal colours, known after 1945 as Twintone. Some were decorated with floral motifs.

Hand-thrown or moulded?

Production during the 1920s and early 1930s consisted largely of hand-thrown ornamental stonewares. The pottery is particularly associated with floral and bird patterns, usually in harmonious blends of deep, subtle colours under a matt glaze.

Many Poole Pottery wares have a characteristic dentil rim or trim, usually in a colour that repeats one of those used in the decoration.

Marks

The firm used a variety of marks: if the base is unmarked, the piece is almost certainly not Poole. Usually the base is impressed "Carter Stabler Adams Ltd" or "C.S.A." and includes the decorator's monogram. Some pieces have pattern codes – which are usually two letters. If three letters are shown, the third usually indicates the dominant colour. Few pieces are dated. Few fakes have been identified.

A Poole Pottery vase, designed by Truda Carter. 1934–7 9.75in (25cm) high E

Doulton & Co.

A Royal Doulton figurine of "Negligée", designed by Leslie Harradine, HN1228. 1927–36 5in (12.5cm) high F

1. Is the piece bone china?
2. Is the decoration hand-painted with a high-gloss glaze?
3. Is the subject a realistic "modern" woman?
4. Does the figure have an "English rose" type of face (youthful, with fair colouring, a healthy-looking rounded face, and rosy cheeks)?
5. Is the subject shown in a casual pose or situation?
6. Is the piece marked?

Doulton & Co. (British 1815–present)

Figurines formed the staple output of the factory's decorative wares during the 1920s and 1930s. Produced primarily for the British market, most have a characteristic "English rose" look.

Most Doulton figurines of the period are depicted full length; head and shoulder busts, like the one below right, are relatively uncommon. The casual pose is especially typical: Doulton ladies are also shown reclining on sofas, and in other informal situations – a style that would have been considered avant-garde in its day.

Most of the subjects are shown in the context of their new-found freedom. This is often reflected by the costumes – for example, elegant evening gowns or negligées (see opposite). Others wear carnival costume, which is particularly evocative of the 1920s.

Figurines often wear costumes of one bold principal colour.

Condition

The exposed limbs are especially susceptible to being chipped or broken: look for subtle changes in skin tones and surface glazes. Enamels, particularly the blacks, were unstable and prone to flaking, and should be examined for signs of overpainting.

The bases sometimes show stress cracks. This need not unduly trouble the prospective purchaser as long as they don't extend more than 1in (2.5cm) from the hole underneath the base or extend to the visible areas of the piece.

Figures were often mounted on table-lamp bases; these bases are not especially desirable and may be removed. However, this should always be done professionally.

Marks

The figures are usually painted on the base with the words "Potted by Royal Doulton", and those from the 1920s and 1930s have a hand-painted title (as opposed to the printed mark used in the post-war period). They also carry an "HN" number – the factory reference number that gives the title and records when the piece was introduced and withdrawn. Reprints of contemporary catalogues provide information on individual items.

*A Royal Doulton figure, "Gladys", HN 1740.
1935–49 5in (12.5cm) wide H*

113

Carlton ware

A 1920s Carlton ware ginger jar, with "Floral Comets" pattern. 5.25in (13cm) high H

1. Is the decoration hand-painted?
2. Is the shape inventive, and perhaps futuristic?
3. Is a dramatic effect achieved through the juxtaposition of bright colours?
4. Is the design geometric, perhaps with formalized flower heads or brocade-type motifs?
5. If the piece is a vase, is it less than 12in (30.5cm) tall, and if a bowl, is it less than that in diameter?
6. Is the piece signed "Carlton ware" in script?

Carlton ware (British, 1890–1992)

Carlton ware was produced by the Carlton Works at Stoke, between 1890 and 1957, the pottery division of Wiltshaw and Robinson. It was renamed Carlton Ware Ltd in 1958. Production ended in 1992.

Types of ware

Ceramics produced during the 1920s and 1930s fall into three categories:

- geometric design work
- exotically coloured lustre art pottery
- moulded tableware and novelty items such as leaf-shaped dishes in the form of leaves.

Shapes and decoration

The firm simultaneously used a wide variety of forms, including some very popular, inventive Modernist shapes and more traditional items. Colours tend to be bright. From c.1935 softer tones and pastels were used in preference to bolder shades. Some pieces incorporate silver lustre for a dramatic effect. The decoration is hand-painted, often featuring stylized flowers.

Lustre wares

Carlton lustre is generally on a cobalt blue ground, sometimes allied with a mottled tangerine-coloured matt glaze. Decorative features include butterflies, chinoiserie, and naturalistic flora.

A Carlton ware "Tutankhamun Tomb" pattern jar and cover. 1922 12.5in (32cm) high D

Carlton used as many as 12 colours for its lustre ware, many of them dark.

Collecting

Very much the rarest, as well as the best and thus the most collectable, of the Carlton pieces, are the geometric designs, followed by the chinoiserie-style lustre pieces. The more mundane leaf-moulded items, which accounted for most of Carlton's output in the 1920s and 1930s, were made in greater numbers and are less collectable.

Marks

Individual designers are not identified; pieces carry the words "Carlton ware" in script. Some bear the patent word "AUST."

Lenci

*A 1930s Lenci figure,
"Nella", designed by
Helen König Scavini.
9in (23cm) high E*

1. Is the subject female?
2. Are the figures idealized?
3. Do the women have either serene, or coy, coquettish expressions?
4. Is the decoration hand-painted?
5. Is there a smooth semi-matt finish in white or flesh tones?
6. Is the figure wearing a hat, possibly depicted as straw?
7. Are the painted eyebrows exaggerated?

Lenci workshops (Italian, 1919–present)

The Lenci workshops in Turin produced a mixture of stylish and kitsch glazed earthenware and porcelain figures. Most are single subjects; groups are less common. Lenci also made a number of wall masks, and in the 1930s produced a series of highly colourful caricatures.

Many Lenci figures are very modern for their period: to show a langorous woman reclining in an armchair (such as the one on p.118) would have been highly innovative at the time. Typically for Lenci women who are clothed, this figure is depicted in chic contemporary dress.

- Lenci occasionally took some artistic licence with its portrayal of the human form – note the impossible length of the girl's arms in the piece shown opposite.

- Kitsch features might include a frog sitting on the back of a bench (see figure opposite).

- The imagery of some Lenci figures is emphatically that of the 1920s or 1930s, such as this sporty and fashionably dressed girl skier (see right).

- Not all Lenci figures have recognizably period features, although even those that do not, display a combination of naïveté and sophistication that is characteristic of the period.

A 1930s Lenci "Ski" figure. 17in (43cm) high E

A Lenci "Primo Romanzo" figure, by Helen König Scavini. 1936 9.75in (25cm) high D

A c.1930s Lenci "Sul Mondo" figure, by Mario Sturani and Helen König Scavini. 19in (48cm) high C

Recognition points

- Hair is often very blond, almost impossibly yellow as in the two figures on this page.
- Hats, especially straw ones, feature prominently and may be highly exaggerated as in the beret worn by the woman on p.116.

Glazes

A feature of Lenci figures is the use of combined glazes on a single piece – for example, many have matt subjects on a shiny gloss base.

Collecting

Some of the most collectable Lenci figures are those that depict the "new women" of the Art Deco period, particularly those dressed in highly fashionable clothes, playing sports, travelling by train, and so on.

Marks

Lenci figures sometimes come with paper labels identifying the factory; individual designers usually remained anonymous. There are various marks for the Lenci workshops. Sometimes the single word "Lenci" is painted on the figure. Alternatively, the mark "Lenci MADE IN ITALY TORINO" may be found.

Collectors should note that on some signed pieces, the word "Lenci" reads backwards – the result of having been set in positive rather than reverse in the mould.

A Royal Dux figure of two dancers. 13in (33cm) high H

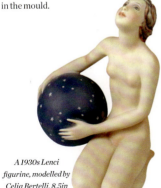

A 1930s Lenci figurine, modelled by Celia Bertelli. 8.5in (21.5cm) high G

ROYAL DUX (Bohemian, 1860–present)

The Royal Dux factory in Bohemia produced some figures that were similar to those of Lenci: they used matt glazes and depicted lean, leggy women, often nudes or in revealing costumes. These figures tend to have more in common with the stylized creations that are associated with the 1920s and 1930s.

Goldscheider

A Goldscheider "Butterfly Dancer" figure, by Josef Lorenzl. c.1923 18.25in (46.5cm) high E

1. Is the costume exotic?
2. Are the colours rich and boldly contrasted?
3. Is any hair in ringlets and glazed in bright colours?
4. If a mask, is it terracotta and partly hollowed at the back?
5. If figures are included, are they very stylized?
6. Are eyes narrow, perhaps half-closed or downcast?
7. Is the piece marked?

Goldscheider (Austrian, 1885–1963)

The firm made figures, wall masks, and large earthenware sculptures, and during the 1920s and 1930s also produced plaster and ceramic versions of the bronzes of Lorenzl (see pp.146–7), Zach (see pp.148–51), and other major sculptors. Some pieces were made for export to the United States.

Figures

In the early 1920s the most popular pieces were lithe, somewhat idealized figures mostly in period attire, often a couple dancing.

Masks

Wall masks (see p.122) were popular in the Art Deco period and made by several companies, but those by Goldscheider are considered very desirable. The firm made a series of six or more designs, all of the same size; these are hand-painted and have a sculpted look. Serene, stylized facial expressions are coupled with bright colours, typically using lots of iron red and yellow. The range also included a few African studies.

Condition

The soft terracotta from which the masks are made is prone to chipping, and paint can also wear: check that it has not been retouched. The back plate should carry the transfer-printed mark.

Two Goldscheider dancers, by Stefan Dakon.
c.1940 13.5in (34cm) high E

A Goldscheider figure of a girl with a dog, by
Stefan Dakon. c.1939 13.25in (33.5cm) high F

A Goldscheider harem dancer, by Josef Lorenzl. c.1927 18.5in (47cm) high E

Staffordshire Goldscheider

In the late 1930s the rights to produce Goldscheider figures were taken up by the Staffordshire company Myott, Son & Co. Ltd, whose versions were marked "Goldscheider made in England". These are not as sought after as the Austrian versions. Goldscheider set up its own British pottery in 1946, and pieces from this period have a signature mark.

Marks

Pieces after 1918 have a transfer-printed mark, "Goldscheider Wien. Made in Austria", which superseded the earlier, pre-war mark of an embossed rectangular pad of a kneeling figure from Greek pottery. Commissioned wares sometimes carry the name of the designer as well, and a serial number. A few are still found with their original paper label.

A Goldscheider ceramic wall mask with mask. c.1932 8.75in (22cm) high G

Rosenthal (Bavarian, 1879–present)

Collectable, fine-quality ceramic figures were produced by the art department at the Rosenthal factory, which also made tablewares, and was noted for its responsiveness to contemporary tastes. Pieces use inventive shapes and tend to be ornate in form or pattern.

Rosenthal figures have an individual, sculptural quality – seen clearly in this piece from c.1930 (see below) – which gradually became more stylized through the 1920s and 1930s. Dancers were also depicted, often wearing colourful, exotic, or futuristic costumes.

Rosenthal also produced a range of cabinet objects, including animals and stylized figures in white.

Collecting

Rosenthal work is relatively underrated: it is probably the nearest equivalent to work by the German factory Meissen, but is more affordable. The figures are more desirable than the tablewares, which are not considered to be very desirable, unless decorated or designed by a leading artist.

Marks

Pieces are incise-marked with the designer's name on the side of the base, and have printed green crossed roses and crown marks underneath.

A Rosenthal figure, by Schwartzkopff. c.1930 10.75in (27.5cm) high F

Cowan Pottery

A Cowan "New Year's Eve in New York City" by Viktor Schreckengost,
otherwise known as the "Jazz Bowl". 1930 14in (35.5cm) diam A

1. Is any painted decoration applied by hand and highly stylized, with a minimal use of colour?
2. Are glazes well applied?
3. Is the modelling of figural work well executed?
4. If earthenware, is the body pale buff in colour?
5. If porcelain, is the body white?
6. If a statuette, is it slipcast, with a hollow body?
7. Is the piece marked?

Cowan Pottery (American, 1913–31)

This works was founded by Reginald Guy Cowan, who produced most of the early designs. In 1927 it expanded to include the Cowan Pottery Studio Inc. and over the next four years it produced its most advanced designs by designers including Waylande Gregory, Edward and Thelma Frazier Winter, and Paul Manship. The limited edition "studio" lines are highly collectable.

Style

Holloware, statuettes, and other items are slipcast with a monochrome glaze, although polychrome statuettes in a bright, unnaturalistic palette are found.

The Viktor Schreckengost "Jazz Bowl"

Schreckengost specialized in ceramic decoration in a sophisticated, modern, American style. Some of his work was produced by Cowan, and his best-known design is the "Jazz" punchbowl, opposite. It was designed in 1930, and made in an edition of 50, each slightly different. Jazz wares are decorated using the sgraffito technique, with images symbolic of Jazz Age New York.

Marks

Pieces by Guy Cowan are typically marked with the name "Cowan" moulded in relief, sometimes with a monogram "R G" below. Most products bear impressed, relief-moulded, or printed marks, sometimes including the artist's name or monogram. The word "Lakeware" is impressed on some flower vases (made for florists) between 1927 and 1931.

Wilhelm Hunt Diederich (American, 1884–1953)

Another craftsman working in a consciously modern American style was Hungarian-born Diederich, who emigrated to the United States in 1899. His work includes graphic and textile designs, although he is best known for his metalwork. He developed an interest in ceramics following a trip to North Africa in 1923. For the next decade he produced decorative earthenware with a rustic flavour. Large dishes, thickly potted and glazed and decorated with earth tones on a white ground are characteristic.

A Wilhelm Hunt Diederich faïence bowl. c.1930
15in (38cm) diam D

Other ceramics

A 1930s Gustavsberg Pottery Argenta vase, by Wilhelm Kåge. 8in (20.5cm) high F

There are many attractive tablewares in period colours and patterns, available today relatively inexpensively because they are unmarked, not by major craftsmen, or not quite as finely executed as the wares shown on the previous pages. There are also a number of novelty items on the market. Perhaps the most popular of these was the tea service in the form of a thatched cottage. Other novelty pieces include teapots in the form of racing cars, usually bearing the registration plate "T42 OK", and aeroplanes.

A Theodore Haviland Limoges porcelain parrot, by Edouard Sandoz. c.1920 7.5in (19cm) high H

A large number of factories, some of which survived for only a few months, made tea sets for the masses, especially during the 1930s. Pedigree is usually determined by the type of glaze, the shape, and the way the decoration complements the shape. Many borrow from the work of major designers, but misinterpret the style: the design may be a little heavy in form and is not equally successful on each piece (unlike designs by Clarice Cliff, which work in many different scales). The earthenware body may be of a similar quality to that of more expensive pieces.

• Pieces were made inexpensively by combining mass-produced blanks with mass-produced patterns.

• Most ceramics of the period are signed, but the signature or factory mark is by no means a guarantee of quality or value. The Staffordshire Myott, Son & Co. pottery made decorative wares reminiscent of those by Clarice Cliff. Typical designs, like the one opposite above, use hand-painted bold areas of the

A 1930s Myott "Beaky" jug. 9in (23cm) high H

autumnal colours popular in the Art Deco period.

Dressing table wares with figural tops were popular in the 1920s and 1930s. There are many types, varying in size from ½in (1.2cm) to around 4in (10cm). Any contemporary-looking figure in porcelain is worth looking at as they command a premium.

At the Swedish Gustavsberg factory, artistic director Wilhelm Kåge (1889–1960) produced the Art Deco Argenta range from 1929 to 1952. It used electrolysis to build silver on stoneware. Argenta ware has gained in popularity, but is still relatively inexpensive.

Silver deposit on tablewares was also used by Lennox in New York, but with more traditional forms and decoration.

The Danish manufacturer, Bing & Grøndahl, produced simple, tasteful shapes such as vases with upright rectangular panel forms, sometimes with small shoulder handles. Form and decoration are invariably well balanced, and pieces are hand-finished, always against the same mottled jade green semi-matt glaze.

Noritake (Japanese/American, 1904–present)

Noritake produced hand-painted porcelain on a scale that could compete with printed designs. During the 1920s and 1930s the design team was based in New York. The adventurous, and now most collectable designs, were produced in Japan and reimported to the United States, which was its major market. Wares for the British market included hand-painted designs of Arab encampments, and lavish tea and decorative wares reminiscent of 18thC styles, many with gilt decoration.

Marks

Wares are marked on the base, usually with the words "NORITAKE" and "MADE IN JAPAN". The trademark has undergone many changes and collectors should familiarize themselves with the appropriate marks for the period.

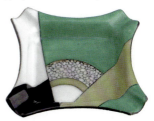

A 1930s Noritake geometric ashtray. 4.5in (11.5cm) wide H

SCULPTURE

By the beginning of the 20thC, sculpture had become a very expensive art form beyond the means of most people. Spelter figures, introduced in an attempt to undersell more expensive bronze examples, served only to debase commercial sculpture. The Art Deco years saw the rebirth of sculpture, especially in bronze, as an art form for the masses. Before the First World War, pieces were produced as one-off art objects, but the introduction in the late 1920s of mass-production techniques allowed larger quantities to be made. France was the main centre of production, followed by Germany and Austria. German figures tend towards athletic, futuristic types; French work is more evocative of the frivolous side of the Jazz Age.

Women are the most common subject. They are often athletic or Amazonian, as in the work of Marcel Bouraine (see pp.142–3). Futuristic and theatrical elements, exemplified by the work of Demêtre Chiparus (see pp.136–9), are common, and figures are often shown performing modern activities, such as smoking. Erotic subjects, such as those of Bruno Zach (see pp.148–51), are especially collectable; historical figures are less keenly sought after. Sporting subjects are popular, as are pierrots and pierrettes. Children as subjects also made a revival during this period.

Exotic animals, especially those of a sleek and speedy nature, were often featured. Several French sculptors made sea and other birds with a novelty element in the design – for example, a bird in flight would be supported by the tip of a wave. Panthers, gazelles, and deer were common, often pursued by Diana-type figures.

The main materials were bronze and chryselephantine – a novel combination of bronze and ivory popularized in the 1920s. Figures in this medium tend to be more

A Franz Hagenauer brass figure of a cat, designed c.1930. 10in (25.5cm) long F

A Demêtre Chiparus chryselephantine figure of the Assyrian queen, Semiramis.
c.1925 26.5 in (67.5cm) high AA

*A bronze and
ivory figure, by
Ferdinand Preiss,
designed c.1925.
13.75in (35cm)
high A*

sought after than pieces entirely in either ivory or bronze, and therefore command a premium. The more ivory used, the more expensive the piece is overall.

Many sculptures were subjected to metallic patination. Gilt and silvered patination were the most favoured, and green was the most popular coloured variety. Patination that has worn away – through age or over enthusiastic cleaning – will be detrimental to value.

Bases acquired a greater degree of importance than before the Art Deco period. Green Brazilian onyx, black slate, and cream striated marble were the most popular materials and are usually carved into geometric shapes.

Figures are usually signed, but not every signed piece is genuine: because of the enormous popularity of Art Deco sculptures, there are many fakes on the market. Period simulated chryselephantine pieces, which are bronzed spelter combined with plastic (often referred to as "ivorene"), can be difficult to identify as the bronze patination can be quite thick. Look underneath and scratch the figure from the inside to check the colour of the metal, which will be yellow if it is genuine bronze, silver if spelter. The development of a technique for graining ivorene faces to resemble ivory makes modern copies harder to identify. Look carefully at the finish: there should be no mould lines. Also check how snug the fit is: ivory has a sharp edge and joins flush with any bronze, while ivorene, which is moulded, tends to chamfer on the corners. Fakes are usually applied to very heavy bases, often of marble, to make the overall piece seem heavier and therefore more authentic.

Genuine sculptures will show signs of natural wear, but many bronze figures have been artificially aged by applying salt to the nuts holding the piece to the base, giving the appearance of rust. Genuine pieces will be neither over-bright nor too rusty.

A 1930s rare, life-size Hagenauer brass sculpture of a waiter. 65in (165cm) high C

Ferdinand Preiss

A Preiss "Champagne-Dancer" bronze and ivory figure. c.1930 16.5in (42cm) high D

1. Is the figure anatomically correct?
2. Is the face naturalistic, and perhaps tinted to suggest, for example, rouge?
3. Do the costumes have a metallic finish?
4. Does it bear the "PK" monogram and a signature?

Ferdinand Preiss (German, 1882–1943)

Most Preiss figures are made of chryselephantine, a combination of bronze and ivory (see p.128). However, Preiss also made all-ivory figures, often small Classical female nudes. The quality of his carving was usually very high. Many of his figures are teutonic, Aryan types with tinted naturalistic faces and stained hair. He specialized in sporting figures, some based on real sportsmen and sportswomen, and actresses. Most Preiss figures are less than 14in (35.5cm) high.

He produced an Aryan figure in which all the parts were carved separately, screwed to the bronze, and individually finished.

Identification point

Most Preiss bases are made of green, black, or a combination of green and striated Brazilian onyx, sometimes banded with black Belgian slate.

Value points

- Preiss figures on ashtrays or dish-mounted tend to be less desirable than figures on bases.
- Preiss's ivory child sculptures are not as desirable as the chryselephantine or female studies.

Beware fakes

As with the work of other top sculptors of the period, copies exist. These often use a softer type of stone that resembles onyx. Be suspicious of any figures attributed to Preiss that have very elaborate bases.

Marks

Figures usually bear the "PK" monogram (for the Preiss-Kassler foundry) and the signature "F. Preiss".

A pair of ivory figures, "Dreaming" by Preiss. c.1925 14in (35.5cm) high D

*A Preiss "Red Dancer", patinated bronze and
ivory figure. c.1925 15in (38cm) high B*

The Preiss-Kassler foundry

The company was formed in Berlin in
1906. Preiss himself designed most of the
models produced by the firm, although
by 1914 there were about six designers
working for the foundry. The factory
closed during the First World War, but
reopened in 1919 and by the middle of
the next decade employed about ten
designers. In 1929 Preiss-Kassler took
over the Rosenthal und Maeder (RuM)
foundry and its sculptors.

Preiss-Kassler sculptors included:
Rudolf Belling, Dorothea Charol,
Walter Kassler, R. W. Lange, Philip
Lenz, Paul Philippe, Otto Poertzel
(see opposite), and Ludwig Walter.

Recreational themes

Figures of the Art Deco period generally
tend to convey a sense of living life
to the full. Many are engaged in what
would have been considered "modern"
activities, often reflecting women's
release from demure stillness and
decorative inactivity. A range of sports
and pastimes were depicted, especially:

• dancing
• snake charming and acrobatics
• swimming/bathing
• smoking
• golf, skiing, and tennis
• skating
• javelin throwing
• fishing.

Prof/Otto Poertzel
(German, 1876–1963)

For many years controversy has surrounded some figures which emanated from the Preiss-Kassler factory and are marked "Prof Poertzel". These bear such a resemblance to the work of Preiss that it was suggested Preiss used the name Poertzel as a pseudonym.

However, it is now believed that Poertzel worked at Preiss's foundry. Poertzel figures are usually chryselephantine and, unlike some by Preiss, seldom appear in all-ivory. Some figures emanating from the Preiss-Kassler foundry bear Preiss's and Poertzel's signature. Although several of these figures are signed by Poertzel, almost identical examples bear Preiss's signature, and other versions feature both names.

Note

It has often been assumed that the dull surface of some patinated figures is caused by dirt. Consequently, many of them have been polished to such an extent that their patinated top surface has been completely rubbed away. This over-cleaning is very detrimental to value.

"Cast from a model by", is a term sometimes used in auction house catalogues to indicate that the figure is not the original model.

An Otto Poertzel "Clown Dance" gilded bronze figure. c. 1925 13.75in (35cm) high G

Demêtre Chiparus

1. Are the costumes elaborate and tight-fitting – for example, cat suits or skullcaps?
2. Does the sculpture have an exotic or science fiction look?
3. Is the pose theatrical?
4. Does the base have a sculptural quality, and perhaps an architectural marble or onyx plinth?
5. Is the material chryselephantine (an expensive and highly desirable combination of bronze and ivory)?
6. Is there an Etling foundry mark?

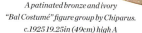

A patinated bronze and ivory
"Bal Costumé" figure group by Chiparus.
c.1925 19.25in (49cm) high A

Demêtre Chiparus (Romanian/ French, 1888–1950)

Although born in Romania, Chiparus worked in Paris. Many of his early figures were produced by the Parisian company, Etling (see p.69). Some later works were produced by the Les Neveux de J. Lehmann (LNJL) foundry. Chiparus was the chief exponent of chryselephantine, a highly desirable combination of bronze and ivory. He specialized in depicting exotic women, many inspired by the Ballets Russes, popular in Paris between c.1917 and c.1929. Inspiration was also provided by other contemporary figures and shows. Many of his sculptures exhibit Mexican, Inca, Aztec, or Mayan influences. Nudes are uncommon. Some pieces were made in more than one size and in both bronze and chryselephantine.

Elaborate bases are typical of Chiparus. Many of his sculptures also have inset plaques whose motifs echo the theme of the subject.

Condition

This is crucial to any assessment of value; the extremities of many figures have suffered from knocks and chips.

A Chiparus bronze and ivory figure of "The Hoop Girl", designed c.1924. 19in (48cm) high C

Ivory is especially susceptible to being damaged and is also prone to cracking: this is particularly detrimental to value where the cracks extend down the face, giving the piece a disfiguring black-veined appearance.

Beware fakes

Fakes of chryselephantine figures have appeared on the market, including some made of plastic. Examine the following:

• The quality of casting and carving, and the subtlety of joints.

• The graining of any ivory (although fakes made from artificially grained plastic or "ivorene" have appeared).

• The facial tint; this should be subtle, possibly showing signs of age. Be suspicious of garish, modern-looking paint, but don't rule it out altogether – the sculpture may have been retouched.

• The gilt surface, which should have acquired a patination, is hard to reproduce artificially.

A Chiparus "Chained Dancer" carved ivory and bronze figure.
c.1925 12.5in (32cm) high B

- The original figures were sometimes secured to the base by wing nuts; the fakes invariably use an ordinary screw and nut.

Marks

Chiparus nearly always signed his work on the base. Signatures may include "D. H. Chiparus" and the inscription "ETLING. PARIS".

A Chiparus "Vested Dancer" patinated bronze and ivory figure. c.1925 21.5in (54.5cm) high B

A Chiparus "Dancer of Kapurthala" bronze and ivory figure. c.1925 22in (56cm) high B

C. J. R. Colinet

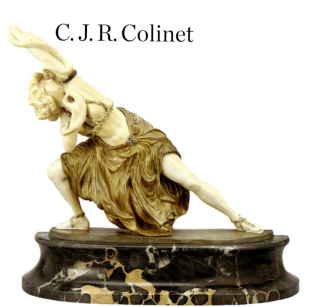

*An ormolu and ivory figure of the "Dance of Carthage",
by Colinet. c.1930 12.25in (31cm) high B*

1. Is the costume flowing and elaborate?
2. Does the figure embody a strong sense of movement?
3. Does the sculpture have an Eastern flavour?
4. Is the subject idealized?
5. Are women generously proportioned (in contrast to the more
   streamlined figures of Chiparus, see pp.136–9)?
6. Do women convey a sense of the *femme fatale*?

**Claire-Jeanne-Roberte Colinet
(Belgian/French, c.1880–1950)**

Colinet is mainly known for her series of dancers. Several versions were made of the same figure. For example, the "Ankara Dancer" was made with and without a pair of brass leggings, on different coloured marble bases, and in different sizes, such as 13 and 24in (33 and 61cm) high, and carried different signatures, including: inscribed simply "Cl.J.R. Colinet 13"; "C.J.R. Colinet" and stamped "42 Made in France"; and impressed with the LNJL foundry seal.

In addition to dancers, Colinet depicted a number of mythical and historic figures, such as "Narcissus", "Cupid", "Joan of Arc", and a crusader. These are less collectable and therefore less expensive.

Dancers of the world

Each dancer has a title plaque. The bas relief on the base often reflects the nationality of the dancer, usually a dramatic, idealized figure. Dancers often hold an emblem typical of the country they represent, such as the sombrero brandished by the "Mexican Dancer". Other figures in the series include the "Hindu Dancer", "Theban Dancer", "Oriental Dancer", and the "Egyptian Dancer". Most of the dancers are of chryselephantine,

*A Colinet "Spanish Dancer", patinated
bronze and ivory figure.
c.1930 19in (48cm) high E*

with a gilt or cold-painted surface, or a combination of the two. Bases are either onyx or marble, or, very occasionally, alabaster. This "Spanish Dancer" (see above) is unusual in being of patinated bronze. Fakes are known to exist.

It is not known precisely how many dancers were in the series, as new ones are still being identified.

Marcel-André Bouraine

A Bouraine bronze and ivory group of a satyr with maiden. c.1925 18.5in (47cm) high D

1. Is the subject a figure from history or mythology, or a dancer or clown?
2. Is the pose exaggerated and dramatic, perhaps with the subject depicted balanced on one leg?
3. Is the figure of bronze or chryselephantine?
4. Is there a multimedia effect, with elaborate appliqué details?
5. Is there a sense of muscular strength or windswept movement?
6. Is there an elaborate base, perhaps of streaked or patinated black marble? (Onyx, brass, and bronze were also common.)
7. Does the piece bear a signature on the base or plinth, and the inscription of the Etling foundry in Paris?

Marcel-André Bouraine (French, 1886–1948)

Bouraine is best known for his chryselephantine figures, made during the interwar years, and for his groups cast fully in bronze. Amazons were popular, as were sporting and mythical figures. Some wear two-dimensional formalized draperies. Many others are nude. Groups often contain animal as well as human figures, especially hunting dogs, swans, or other birds.

Bouraine's sculptures are distinctive for their use of a variety of media combined in one piece. Patinas of gold and bronze were often employed, some including enamelled, silvered, or stencilled surfaces, and garlanded with carved, sometimes painted ivory.

Many Bouraine figures are portrayed with outstretched arms and holding a prop, such as a hoop, bow, spear, or, as with this dancer of the 1920s (see right), a fan.

- The complicated, partially stepped, marble plinth supporting "The Fan Dancer" is typical.
- A recurring subject in Bouraine's work was the streamlined, naked Amazonian figure or Diana-like huntress, with windswept hair, frozen in the motion of running, hunting, or throwing a spear.
- Some figures were made in more than one size and with minor variations.

Marks

Bouraine sculptures are usually marked. Much of his work was commissioned and distributed by the Parisian firm Etling (see p.69). Marks on one figure might consist of a stamped "BRONZE FRANCE", signed "BOURAINE", an inscribed "ETLING. PARIS" and an inscribed "MADE IN FRANCE".

No fakes are known to exist. The French glass artist Joseph-Gabriel Argy-Rousseau (see pp.62–3) created statuettes in *pâte-de-verre* during the 1930s after his designs.

A Bouraine silvered and cold-painted bronze figure, "The Fan Dancer". c.1925 17in (43cm) high E

Pierre Le Faguays

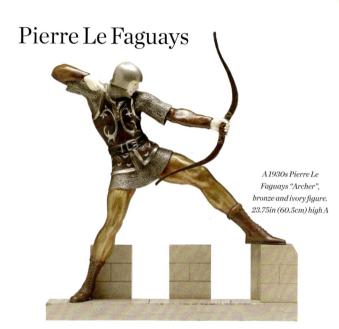

A 1930s Pierre Le Faguays "Archer", bronze and ivory figure. 23.75in (60.5cm) high A

1. Is the figure delicately poised, or simplified and serene?
2. Is the material bronze, possibly silvered or combined with ivory?
3. Is the human form precisely and accurately sculpted?
4. Does the bronze have a damascened pattern similar to that used by Bouraine (see pp.142–3.)?
5. Is the subject a single figure?
6. Is the base in black striated marble, or black and green onyx?
7. Is the piece marked "Le Faguays" or "Fayral"?

Pierre Le Faguays (French, 1892–1935)

Le Faguays, who was also known as "Fayral", produced work for Arthur Goldscheider's Parisian foundry in the 1920s, and exhibited under Goldscheider's "La Stele" label at the Paris Exhibition in 1925. He also worked for the house of Le Verrier.

He worked in three distinct idioms. The most successful and desirable of these is his female studies, which have a strong element of stylization. Typically, there is a distinct feeling of stillness and serenity, with the limbs held close to the body – a style that is very different from that of other craftsmen working in this period. Others depict the more conventional Art Deco woman – often nude or scantily clad, and shown dancing or as a harem girl or warrior. The third distinct group is that depicting idealized historical figures, such as this archer (see left).

Materials

Many of Le Faguays' sculptures and most of the larger ones are in bronze; smaller pieces may include ivory. He also worked in wood, stone, and silvered bronze. All-ivory figures are rare. Some pieces use cold-painted colours.

- The bases are in a variety of materials; black striated marble and black and green onyx were popular.

Collecting

Although Le Faguays was relatively prolific, his work does not come up for sale as frequently as pieces by other sculptors. Some of his pieces incorporate jardinières or are fitted with electricity for lighting and these command a premium (as do any items with a utilitarian as well as a decorative value). The largest group – the dancers and harem figures – which represents Le Faguays' more commercial side, are perhaps slightly less sought after and were not made in large numbers.

Marks

The sculptures are usually signed "Le Faguays" or "Fayral". This may be carved or incise-cast in the base. Some bear the foundry mark "LNJL Paris", and may carry a design number. Pieces displayed at the 1925 Paris Exhibition carry the "La Stele" foundry seal as well as Le Faguays' name.

A 1930s Pierre Le Faguays patinated bronze figure, "Locomotion". 26in (66cm) wide E

145

Josef Lorenzl

1. Is the figure stylized, with a dramatic posture?
2. Are the limbs unnaturally elongated to suggest elegance, rather than being strictly accurate?
3. Is the subject female, and either naked or in skin-tight clothing?
4. Is she poised on one leg, possibly with an outstretched arm?
5. Does the sculpture stand on a pedestal?
6. Is the base onyx?
7. Is the piece signed?

A bronze figure "Speed" by Lorenzl.
c.1930 12in (30.5cm) high E

Josef Lorenzl (Austrian, 1892–1950)

Lorenzl produced a range of figures in bronze, ivory, and occasionally in chryselephantine (see p.128). His sculptures usually depict single females, and tend to be small – up to 12in (30.5cm) without the pedestal. Unusually for sculptors of the period, he seldom depicted figures from antiquity or the theatre. However, his females have the 1920s or 1930s look, with bobbed or cropped hair. They tend to be very slim with streamlined figures and small breasts and are usually idealized, although the facial features are realistic, with serene, calm expressions. The nudes often hold a scarf, fan, or other accessory. Many of the subjects are dancers shown in acrobatic positions.

- Lorenzl favoured a patinated silver or gilt finish with enamel on the scarves, hair, and so on. This gives the figures their characteristic metallic look.
- Figures were produced in a range of sizes. The bases are usually faceted and of plain onyx, although black slate and marble were used.
- Plaster and ceramic versions of Lorenzl bronzes (and those of other important sculptors of the day) were produced by the Austrian firm Goldscheider (see pp.120–2)
- Lorenzl's work has been faked and copied.

Signatures

Lorenzl used a variety of signatures. The most common include:

- "Lorenzl" in full, which is the most common of his signatures.
- "Lor", on small pieces, when it is usually found under the skirt or under the foot.
- "Renzl".
- The painted mark "Crejo" appears on some partially painted figures.
- Script lettering is commonly used on taller pieces, generally on the base.
- Capital letters, usually on smaller pieces, are found on the perimeter of the flat base.

A gilt-bronze and ivory figure by Lorenzl.
c.1930 12.5in (32cm) high E

Bruno Zach

1. Is the subject risqué?
2. If a woman, is the figure semi-naked, with an Amazonian expression?
3. Do women have hair that is bobbed or tied with a bow?
4. Is there a sense of movement to any clothes, which may also be in a contrasting patination?
5. Does the subject have an idealized figure?
6. Is the base of fairly plain black or grey marble with fine cream striations?
7. Is there an incised signature cast into the top of the base?

A green and gilt patinated bronze figure "The Riding Crop" by Zach. c.1930 13in (33cm) high AA

A Zach gilt and enamel cold-painted bronze figure of a semi-clad lady, with fencing sword. c.1925 28in (71cm) high B

Bruno Zach (Austrian, 1891–1935)

Little is known of the life of this sculptor, famous for his erotic, slightly prurient portraits of the Berlin demi-monde. It is believed that Zach was born in Ukraine and studied at the Academy of Fine Arts in Vienna. Among his lesser known works are some sporting figures, such as skiers, which are not as collectable as the erotic subjects he is best known for.

Stance and costume

Zach's subjects are nearly always female. Multiple figures are rare, but pairs exist, usually of dancers or lovers. The women often hold riding crops or whips; most subjects stand with their legs slightly apart in an affirmative stance, rather than in the ladylike pose typical of many figures of the Art Deco period. These are not the jewel-adorned playthings often depicted in the 1920s and 1930s, but have a certain severity uncharacteristic of sculptures at the time. It is not uncommon for Zach's dancing figures to be shown poised on one leg.

Zach accurately depicted the costume of the period. This is helpful for dating, as pyjama suits and camisoles were not introduced until c.1920.

A Zach silvered and patinated bronze figure of a female archer. c.1925 15in (38cm) high E

A Zach patinated bronze figure of a girl, dated. 1929 16in (40.5cm) high D

Materials

Zach worked mostly in bronze or chryselephantine. He favoured gilt patination, and very occasionally used patinated bronze. Ivory was often

The costumes also contribute to the sensual impression given by the figures – for example, garters, and full length gloves (although these are not useful for dating his work, as they were worn from the end of the 19thC).

Some of Zach's figures wear leather clothing, and most of them are shown wearing shoes or boots – even if they are otherwise naked or scantily clad.

A Zach cold-painted and gilt-bronze and ivory figure. c.1925 26in (66cm) high AA

contrasted with black patination. He also made a few cold-painted pieces.

Fakes and copies
Copies of Zach's work abound: these are distinguished by their poor-quality casting and patination. The figures tend to have an ungraceful, almost dumpy silhouette, and are neither sensual nor erotic. The proportions of the body appear wrong, the posture awkward and unflattering, and the costume static. The bases are usually thinner than those used for genuine Zach figures, and the pedestals may be green onyx, which was rarely used by Zach.

Signatures
Zach's work is nearly always signed with his big bold signature. Some unsigned pieces have been attributed to him, but unless the piece is marked it should not be accepted as Zach without contemporary documentation.

Cold-painted or metallic patination?
Cold-painting, popularized by Franz Bergman, was largely an Austrian practice. Whereas most Art Deco figures of the period were finished with a metallic patination, obtained by exposing the metal to the fumes of various chemicals, Bergman used coloured enamels, which were annealed or painted onto the figure.

A bronze of a young lady, "Florette", by Bruno Zach. c.1925 16in (40.5cm) high C

The Hagenauer Workshop

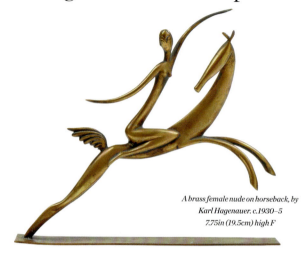

*A brass female nude on horseback, by
Karl Hagenauer. c.1930–5
7.75in (19.5cm) high F*

1. Are any figures stylized and streamlined?
2. Are animal and human faces almost mask like?
3. Is the sculpture made of silver, chromium-plated bronze, or brass?
4. Do any figures or animals combine flowing curves with clean angles and elongated tapering limbs?
5. Is the sculpture self-supporting or mounted on a minimal base?
6. Is the surface smooth without embellishment?
7. Do animal and human forms display a sense of movement?
8. Is the monogram "wHw" stamped onto the base, or, if there is no base, on the underside of the body?

Hagenauer (Austrian, 1898–1987)

The Hagenauer Werkstätte (Workshop) was founded in Vienna in 1898 by Carl Hagenauer (1872–1928). Hagenauer had trained as a goldsmith. Initially, it specialized in practical and ornamental artefacts – metal tablewares, lamps, mirrors, and vases – but it became famous for the metal figurines and groups of the 1910–30 period, which were exhibited throughout Europe.

Carl Hagenauer's eldest son Karl (1898–1956) joined the firm in 1919 and, together with his brother Franz (1906–86), took over in 1928. In the 1930s their designs were at the forefront of the New Realism. Hagenauer designs were influenced by the work of the Wiener Werkstätte (see pp.176–7).

Note

Wood and bronze was a favourite combination in figures from c.1910 until the mid-1920s. Pieces from this period were of an avant-garde, highly stylized design, becoming more realistic and detailed in the 1930s.

A Karl Hagenauer figure of a wood and brass deer. c.1930 11.75in (30cm) long F

A Hagenauer ebonized wood polar bear,
sesigned 1930s. 5in (12.5cm) long G

Form and decoration

The movement of the piece, whether human or animal, is conveyed by simple unbroken design, pared of superfluous detail. Form often merges into function: horse-riders into lampstands, arms and hands into brackets for candelabra. The decoration is also contained within the form, rather than applied to it.

Sculptures are usually of bronze, copper, or brass, a wood (often ebony) and metal combination, or chrome.

Collecting

It is difficult to distinguish between the work of the three principal Hagenauers. However, Carl and Karl were largely responsible for the utilitarian wares, while Franz specialized in decorative sculptures.

A 1930s Hagenauer patinated bronze figure
of an African woman. 17in (43cm) high E

Hagenauer masks are particularly sought after, as well as those figures with a Modigliani or Brancusi influence. Usually, the more decorative and stylish the piece, the more collectable it is.

Marks
The pieces are usually stamped with the Hagenauer monogram "wHw" and sometimes the designer's name, the date, and place of origin.

A 1930s Hagenauer wood and silvered bronze figure of a Spanish dancer. 12.5in (32cm) high F

A 1920s Hagenauer wood and bronze sculpture. 14in (35.5cm) high G

François Pompon

A Pompon carved plaster maquette of a polar bear.
c.1923 12in (30.5cm) wide F

1. Is the piece stylized?
2. Is the surface smooth?
3. Does the patination complement the subject?
4. Is the subject an animal?
5. Is the figure freestanding?
6. Does the form convey a sense of movement?
7. Is the piece signed?

François Pompon (French, 1855–1933)

Pompon was one of the leading animaliers of the period. He created a number of important animal sculptures, including a polar bear (see opposite) – his most famous sculpture – exhibited at the 1922 Paris Exhibition when he was 67. Pompon's work was highly stylized. He paid particular attention to the finish, making good use of patination. Surfaces were often highly polished. Although his figures are so stylized, Pompon nevertheless managed to suggest a sense of movement. It is not unusual for Pompon's animals to be freestanding, although most animal sculptures of the period have marble bases.

Marks

His work is usually signed underneath with the word "POMPON". Few fakes are known.

A Pompon cast bronze sculpture of a stylized owl. c.1927 7in (18cm) high E

Edouard Marcel Sandoz (Swiss, 1881 1971)

After Pompon, Sandoz is probably the most important animalier of the period (his monuments and portraits are generally regarded as works of lesser importance). He favoured a more formalized approach. Some of Sandoz's work is unusually small, less than 1.5in (4cm) tall, and appears in glazed porcelain as well as marble. His animals are usually mounted on marble bases.

ART DECO ANIMALS

Certain animals feature strongly in Art Deco sculpture. They include:

- Panthers, the most popular Deco animal, shown singly and in packs.
- Gazelles, second to the panther in popularity, often depicted with Diana, the huntress, or with sea birds.
- Dogs; these exemplify the spirit of the age, particularly borzois.
- Birds, including Oriental pheasants and fantail doves. French sculptures sometimes show gulls on the tip of a wave.
- Fish (especially Lalique).
- Cats, now very collectable.

Other Art Deco animal sculptors

Collectable names include A. Becquerel, Marcel Bouraine , Cornelia Chapin, Alex Kéléty, G. H. Laurent, Max Le Verrier, and Paul Manship.

Other sculpture

The works shown on the preceding pages represent the best sculptures that the period has to offer, and as such they tend to be expensive. However, there is a fair amount of less expensive sculpture on the market. Some of these wares have simply yet to become appreciated; others lack either the technical perfection or the quality of materials that typify the best pieces.

Some relatively inexpensive works are still available in bronze and sometimes even in chryselephantine and these usually represent better value than those sculptures made in

A group of alabaster entwined mermaids.
c.1930 15in (38cm) high H

spelter, a zinc alloy introduced in the early 20thC. However, by the 1920s and 1930s some quite attractive spelter figures were being made.

The forms of many lesser sculptures are simple and employ the minimum of casting – the fingers may not be separated, and feet are often cast as one block. Facial features may be poorly executed, with bland expressions.

Spelter is easily scratched and the white metal often shows through. It also fractures more easily than bronze. Natural wear may cause it to oxidize and form a series of bubbles on the surface, popularly known as "spelter disease". Once these bubbles or fractures occur, they are extremely difficult to repair.

A pair of silvered bronze and ivory figures of children, by Georges Omerth. c.1910 F

Sculptures of children, such as the ones shown opposite below, were popular subjects between 1900 and 1925. Their desirability today is reduced by their limited decorative appeal and their lack of visual drama. This example is not particularly endearing: it is somewhat static and lacks charm. The standard of craftsmanship is not high: the silvering is distressed and worn, and the plate is wearing through. The bases are plain and cheap.

Some attempt has been made to introduce an erotic element into the alabaster figure of two mermaids (see left) but the limbs are unnaturally long and the poses appear uncomfortable.

The spelter figures on this page are thematically in keeping with the period but the poses lack finesse. The one shown top right is

A spelter figure of a dancer with hoops. c.1925 10in (25.5cm) high G

A cold-painted spelter figural lamp, modelled as a semi-nude exotic dancer. c.1930 22in (56cm) high G

somewhat inelegant and conveys little sense of movement. The posture seems unlikely and even absurd. The finish is gaudy and relatively unattractive and the lampshade she is holding is out of proportion with the base. The figure of a dancer holding two hoops (see below left) is more successful, but while the folds of her skirt suggest movement, the hoops she is holding appear to have warped or been otherwise damaged.

Both these dancers recall the work of Lorenzl (see pp.146–7), but they are less accomplished in the following ways:

- the posture is contrived and the faces bland
- there is minimal definition
- the spelter shows poor casting
- patination is poorly controlled
- the bases are very simple in form and made from a plain marble.

METALWORK

The 1920s and 1930s witnessed a new interest in wrought iron as a decorative and functional medium: decorative as a surround for blown glass vases; functional for items such as tables, domestic gates, interior screens, and radiator covers.

The period saw a revival of the craftsmen-metalworkers, the most famous of whom were the Frenchmen Edgar Brandt (1880–1960) (see pp.164–5), who later moved to the United States, Paul Kiss (see p.167), and Louis Majorelle. They often worked in conjunction with other manufacturers – for example, Majorelle made mounts for glass produced by Daum Frères (see pp.58–61). Metalwork was taken to its high point in France by Armand Albert Rateau, who developed exotic bronze furniture cast in a highly individualistic style – for example, a bronze and marble table supported by four stylized pheasants.

At the other extreme, the market was catered for by the creations of the German firm WMF (see pp.168–9), which had been successful with extravagant Art Nouveau and Classical art pewter, but now concentrated on relatively simple forms, often with geometric simulated bronze patination and silvering.

Metal was put to a variety of new uses, especially in France. Several manufacturers used wrought and hammered ironwork as mounts for light fixtures, especially for ceilings. Edgar Brandt made cobra standard lamps (with Daum glass shades) that showed innovative use of bronze as a lighting medium (see p.165).

Fake and reproduction lamps can be found. On an original lamp, the shade and support meet perfectly; the shade and support of a fake are a poor fit and do not make contact. Before making a purchase compare the article with one known to be genuine. Beware of lamps with old wirings and fixtures, as these may have been taken from another old lamp to create an impression of age. Similarly, a perfectly genuine old lamp may well have new wires and fixtures.

Screens were made in metal, often with animal motifs showing creatures popular during the period, such as snakes, gazelles, and pumas. The designer Raymond Subes (see pp.166–7) promoted the use of cast iron allied with plate glass for tables. Some work by Brandt was incorporated into the fittings of the Selfridges department store in London. Much of his work was produced to commission for

A pair of wrought-iron side tables by Paul Kiss, with pink marble tops. 20in (51cm) diam B

*A 1930s "moderne"
floor lamp by
Bel Geddes. 53in
(134.5cm) high E*

important New York buildings. Much
of Subes' work is difficult to identify
as it is incorporated into fixtures, such
as building façades, balustrades, door
frames, furniture mounts, and so on.

The late 1920s and 1930s were the
culmination of the ironwork revival.
Other designers working in wrought
iron at the time were Jules and Michel
Nics, known as Nics Frères. They
specialized in *martelé* (hammered
or planished) surfaces, handmade
furniture, and decorative wares.

Dinanderie, the application of
patinated enamel to non-precious
metals such as copper and steel, was
taken to its peak by Claudius Linossier
and Jean Dunand (see pp.24–5).

The use of spelter was still
widespread; it was employed to a
large extent in sculpture, and in some
instances during the 1920s for car
mascots in chromed metal, made by a
number of artists. Many car mascots,
especially in the United States, were
made for specific models of cars, and
are now very collectable.

Pewter continued to be used for
decorative and practical items – and
inexpensive, simple, geometric,
streamlined pieces were particularly
sought after during the Depression. In
Britain, Liberty adapted its successful
Art Nouveau Tudric range, with its
simulated hammered surfaces, to the

new style. Other pewter manufacturers used Cubistic forms in an attempt to maintain the momentum of growth in the art pewter industry. In Scandinavia, companies produced metalwares that were very Classical in style.

American artists were initially influenced by French metalworkers, but soon began to develop their own styles, working in stainless steel and aluminium on a large scale, and were particularly fond of chrome, using it extensively in interiors and for furniture, friezes, and elevator doors. The International Copper Company patented a nickel-copper alloy, called "Monel" metal, as a popular alternative to aluminium.

Not all metalwork was made to private commission or for the exclusive end of the market: it is still possible to find relatively inexpensive pieces, such as kitchenware and other small household items, especially if they are anonymous or not attributed to major craftsmen.

Condition is important, although rust on ironwork is not a cause for concern: it can be stripped and repainted, as long as the work is done sympathetically. However, some vases have had their patination polished off, and these are rendered almost valueless. Most pieces are signed with a stamp. As yet, very little has been faked or reproduced.

Medallions (small plaques) are one neglected area collectors may find worth pursuing. They tend to be underrated, perhaps because they are neither functional nor do they lend themselves well to display, and they are therefore still modestly priced. Many are commemorative, and include the work of top French sculptors, some of whom, such as Paul Turin and Jean Vernon, specialized in this area. The classic example is the medal produced for the 1925 Exhibition in Paris. Medals are often signed and usually cast in bronze. The condition is very important: dents, scratches, and over-polishing will reduce the value considerably.

In the United States, Norman Bel Geddes (see pp.170–1) was prominent among a group of talented and highly qualified designers, notably Russel Wright, Raymond Loewy, Henry Dreyfuss, and Walter Dorwin Teague (see p.171), who were drawn to industrial design for its artistic and creative potential.

Bel Geddes can be largely credited with creating the streamlined style, which replaced the sharp angles of the 1920s with smooth, sleek rounded forms suggestive of energy and movement. It was a style that was to permeate both interiors and exteriors of buildings, and which proved to be perhaps the most evident form of Art Deco in the United States.

Edgar Brandt

A pair of Brandt bronze cobra andirons, designed c.1925. 13.5in (34cm) long B

1. Is the piece partly or entirely composed of wrought iron, or of cast or silvered bronze?
2. Does an animal form part of the subject?
3. Do the surfaces have a textured appearance?
4. Are the joints and any screws or bolts subtle, or even concealed?
5. Does the piece have ornate decorative elements, such as scrolls or overlapping flower heads?
6. Does the symmetry of the piece seem natural rather than mechanical and rigid?
7. Is the piece stamped "E. Brandt", probably on the footrim?

Edgar Brandt (French, 1880–1960)

Brandt began working in iron at an early age. He made mostly jewellery and wrought ironwork until 1919, when he opened his own atelier in Paris, producing his own designs and those of other designers. His work was acclaimed in 1925, when he co-designed the Porte d'Honneur for the Paris Exhibition, and exhibited his famous five-panel, wrought-iron and brass screen, "Oasis". With its stylized central fountain and French Art Deco-type scrolls, the screen was typical of much of the work Brandt produced during the 1920s. The warm patination and the combination of iron, brass, copper, and other metals were typical.

Wares and styles

Brandt was the leading metalworker of the period both in Paris and New York, where he opened Ferrobrandt Inc., a company that executed commissions for a number of buildings, and also produced a range of domestic wares.

He used the decorative elements of wrought iron to great effect, popularizing the hammered *martelé* finish. Although other metalworkers emulated him, Brandt's work remained technically supreme. In his hands a material of structural purpose became highly decorative, with superbly executed spirals, scrolls, and animals.

As well as industrial commissions, such as railings, grilles, and so on, Brandt produced a range of highly collectable domestic items.

These include:

- radiator covers
- screens
- umbrella stands
- centre tables
- fireplace accessories.

He also made small decorative wares such as jewellery, trays, vases, and paper knives.

Brandt is probably best known for his bronze serpent lamp, "La Tentation", made as a table lamp, a standard lamp, and in an intermediate size. The glass shade was by Daum. Fakes abound. These can usually be detected by the poor quality of the patination; by the lack of definition in the casting of the snake; and by the shades, which are usually of lightweight glass, inferior in quality to the Daum originals.

A Brandt gilt-bronze and Daum
glass "Cobra" lamp.
c.1925 19in (48cm) high B

Raymond Subes

A Subes wrought-iron console table. An almost identical variant of this design was exhibited at the 1925 Paris Exhibition. 50.5in (128cm) wide A

1. Is the piece wrought iron, possibly gilded?
2. Are there floral motifs, possibly stylized?
3. Is any decoration integral with the form?
4. Is the form relatively heavy and durable?
5. Does the piece have a complex form of support?
6. If the form is a table, does it have a large rectangular marble or granite top?

Raymond Subes (French, 1893–1970)

Next to Brandt (see pp.164–5), Subes is probably the most renowned French metalworker of the Art Deco period. In 1919 he became director of the metal workshop of Borderel et Robert, an architectural construction company. Most of his work was on government commissions, notably the SS *Normandie* (see pp.8–9) and other liners. Like Brandt, he initially worked mainly in wrought iron, and occasionally in bronze and copper. By the 1930s his medium had changed to aluminium and oxydized or lacquered steel. Subes pieces coming onto the market are still rarities, and often unsigned.

Form and decoration

Subes' output was prodigious: despite its hand-finished look, his work was mainly mass-produced. His early motifs tend towards to the naturalistic and slightly florid. Iron was finely bent into ribbon- or octopus-like curls, often curving away from a central source. By the end of the 1920s, decoration had become minimal and was often restricted to the supports.

During the 1930s Subes' work became much heavier in appearance. Pieces were often of bronze or aluminium, and employed architectural shapes. Forms are simple and bold. His large 1930s light reflectors were innovative and striking.

Paul Kiss (Romanian/French, 1885–1962)

Like Brandt, Kiss preferred ornate designs and motifs and his work displays keen attention to detail.

As well as wrought iron, he worked in silvered bronze. He is particularly known for his mirrors, which tend to have an elongated form and may include decorative tassels. Other pieces are often mounted or set off by marble, alabaster, or engraved glass. He also made console and mirror sets, table lamps, and ceiling fixtures.

Kiss's work usually has a stamped signature "P. KISS PARIS" or "P. KISS".

A pair of Kiss wrought-iron pedestals. c.1925 38.25in (97cm) high B

WMF Metalwork

1. Does the patinated surface have a slightly rigid appearance?
2. Is it well proportioned and with an attractive finish?
3. Is the decoration burnished or incised?
4. Was it mass-produced from pieces of metal joined by seams?
5. Was the metallic decoration applied by an electrolytic technique?
6. Is it marked WMF?

A WMF patinated brass Ikora vase by Albert Merkle. 1920–30 10in (25.5cm) high H

WMF, Württembergische Metallwarenfabrik (German, 1853–present)

The company emulated the work of French designer Claudius Linossier (1893–1955). Linossier made elegant hammered, chased, and patinated wares. In contrast, WMF used a mass-produced electrolytic technique to apply metallic deposits to metal vases made up of seamed pieces. Surfaces were not textured but patinated, which gives a slightly rigid appearance. Although clearly not handmade, WMF wares are nevertheless well-proportioned, have an attractive finish, and are likely to be within the budget of most collectors.

A number of highly polished examples

A WMF Ikora plate of a dancer with scarves. c.1929 7.25in (18.5cm) diam F

have appeared on the market, the patination having been stripped, often out of ignorance. These vases should be avoided. The 1920s saw the introduction of the Art Deco-styled Ikora metalware, as well as a range of glass that included the iridescent Myra and the heavier Ikora glass, which was decorated with colours and bubbles.

Marks
The WMF mark is distinctive, and is not known to have been faked.

Gantcheff (French, active 1920s)
Another French firm, Gantcheff, made dinanderie wares in Paris in the 1920s. These compare with those made by Linossier for quality and attractiveness. Wares are usually signed on the footrim.

A Fritz August Breuhaus de Groot for WMF sugar bowl. c.1929 6.75in (17cm) high F

Norman Bel Geddes

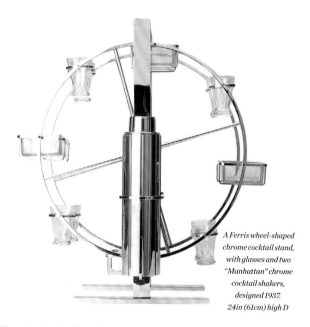

A Ferris wheel-shaped chrome cocktail stand, with glasses and two "Manhattan" chrome cocktail shakers, designed 1937. 24in (61cm) high D

1. Does the design show futuristic elements?
2. Is the design very streamlined?
3. Are there discernible signs of the influence of industrial design?
4. Are the materials and methods of manufacture representative of a Machine Age?

Norman Bel Geddes (American, 1893–1958)

Bel Geddes trained as a theatre and set designer before setting himself up as an industrial designer in 1927. His early commissions, before 1932, were for domestic products, such as gas stoves.

Bel Geddes was the major force behind the streamlined style (see p.163). He declared it treatment suitable for virtually any product, although some of his outlandish ideas for steam locomotives were never realized. Bel Geddes produced metalware for several manufacturers, mostly functional designs, some of which are marked with his facsimile signature. The "Manhattan" cocktail shaker (right), is in chromium-plated metal and was commissioned by the Revere Copper and Brass Company in 1935. Typical of Bel Geddes metalware, it shows a restrained, linear style that complements the streamlined and Skyscraper styles of the 1930s American Art Deco.

A Bel Geddes silver-plated bronze medal for General Motors. 1933 3in (7.5cm) diam E

This commemorative medallion in silver-plated bronze (see above) was created for the 25th anniversary of General Motors in 1933. It has a moulded signature "NORMAN BEL GEDDES" and is stamped "Metallic Art Co. NY". The lettering is in a futuristic typeface and one side of the medallion shows a sleek highly stylized car.

Walter Dorwin Teague (American, 1883–1960)

Another primarily industrial designer, Teague is mainly remembered for the service stations he designed for Texaco in the United States in the mid-1930s. He was retained by the camera company Kodak for about 30 years. He also created a number of successful glass designs for Steuben (see pp.74–5). His work is characterized by a readiness to harmonize function with bold design.

A Bel Geddes Revere "Manhattan" chrome cocktail shaker. 1936–40 13in (33cm) high F

SILVER AND JEWELLERY

One of the most important items of silver produced during this period were tablewares. The emphasis was on form, which tended to be streamlined; decoration took second place or was absent altogether.

The foremost designers were the French, most notably Jean Puiforcat. The Scandinavians, the most famous of whom was Georg Jensen, produced organic, decorated forms, as did the Wiener Werkstätte in Austria. The work of Bauhaus designers, many of whom moved to the United States, was extremely influential. Marianne Brandt, who followed minimalist principles, was regarded as one of the most important Bauhaus silversmiths. American designers also produced some significant work – for example, the cocktail service by Norman Bel Geddes (see pp.170–1), which exemplifies the use of simple perpendicular forms, inspired by the skyscraper (see pp.170–1).

British designers were slow to adopt the new style, and most British silver produced at this time is traditional and undistinguished. Some silversmiths attempted to adopt new ideas, creating engine-turned geometric designs, especially for such items as cigar boxes and pocket cigarette cases.

Guilloche enamel decoration using translucent enamels was especially popular. It was often the only decoration applied to dressing table sets, which tended to be engine-turned designs in silver covered with translucent monochrome enamel.

The luxury end of the jewellery trade was well catered for by all the major manufacturers, among them Cartier, Gerard Sandoz, and Georges Fouquet, who all used Modernist forms, although they also continued to produce pieces in more traditional styles. Exotic jewels were often incorporated, sometimes applied to novelty forms. Chinoiserie was popular, especially in the 1920s, and coral and jade, often carved, became fashionable on a scale not seen before. Glass jewellery was promoted by Lalique (see pp.50–5).

At the other extreme, there was a large amount of mass-produced costume jewellery and metalwork. These designs also made use of the new plastics. Diamanté and marcasite were frequently used, especially in sunbursts or fountain motifs. The lady's wristwatch proved popular, the best examples being French. Watch faces were often silver or platinum inset with geometric initials or paste stones.

A 1920s grape pattern wine coaster, designed by Georg Jensen. 5.5in (14cm) diam E

A Josef Hoffmann silver tea service for Wiener Werkstätte.
c.1917 17.75in (45cm) wide B

Jean Puiforcat

A 1930s Puiforcat silver-plated coffee and tea set, with twin handled tray. The half-reeded canisters have applied silver bead hardwood covers and "C" form handles. Coffee pot 5.5in (14cm) high D

1. Is the form simplified and rounded?
2. Is the surface plain and smooth?
3. Is the piece strongly functional, showing a Cubist influence?
4. Does the piece use materials other than silver on handles or knobs?
5. Are the handles the only decorative elements?
6. Is the surface enlivened by the way in which the large, perfectly smooth areas catch, reflect, and distort light?
7. Are there no visible hammer marks?
8. Is the piece made to a high standard of craftsmanship?
9. Is the style of the object almost futuristic, with glass, wood, or crystal additions?
10. Does the signature bear a French hallmark and the signature "Jean E. Puiforcat"?

Jean Puiforcat (French, 1897–1945)

Puiforcat joined the family firm after the First World War. He concentrated on graceful shapes and rejected traditional embellishments without sacrificing beauty or luxury. Surfaces are usually plain. Even the hammer marks – traditionally the sign of a handmade object – are absent. All his pieces show a high standard of craftsmanship and minute attention to detail.

Puiforcat made functional rather than decorative pieces. In the 1920s he produced tea sets, dishes, and bowls in solid silver and plate, in simple cylindrical or rectangular forms. These are offset by knobs and handles of ivory, jade, lapis lazuli, or hardwood.

In the 1930s his style gave way to purer, sleeker shapes, which are bold statements of form and volume, with occasional touches of ice-green or salmon-pink glass, high-quality wood, or crystal embellishments. These later objects can sometimes appear to be futuristic.

- Some wares also appear as pieces of abstract, Cubist sculpture.
- Tea and coffee sets were mass-produced and survive in large numbers.

- Incomplete sets suffer a disproportionate drop in value.
- All pieces are stamped "Puiforcat" and silver carries a French hallmark.

Christofle (French, 1839–present)

Although it had been cautious in its use of the Art Nouveau style, this family firm was more receptive than Puiforcat to the simplicity and geometricism of Art Deco. It produced all kinds of utilitarian and decorative silverplate. In the 1920s it commissioned pieces from a number of notable designers, including Gio Ponti, Maurice Daurat, Luc Lanel, Süe et Mare, Paul Follot, and Christian Fjerdingstad. Pieces were mass-produced, many in electroplate. This was used for tableware, including some for the SS *Normandie* and other liners.

A 1930s Christofle silver-plated tea and coffee set by Luc Lanel. Tray 19in (48cm) long E

Wiener Werkstätte

An important Josef Hoffmann brass on hammered copper vase or table centrepiece. c.1922 11.5in (29cm) high B

1. Is the design severe and lacking in ornamentation?
2. Alternatively, does the design include berries and leaves?
3. Is it handmade?
4. Does the design incorporate planished (hand-beaten) decoration?
5. Is the shape borrowed from 18thC silver?
6. Is the shape avant-garde?
7. Is the base marked with a monogrammed "P" (for pieces by Pêche) or "JH" (for Hoffmann) and the "WW" monogram?

Wiener Werkstätte (Austrian, 1903–32)

This group of artisans worked in a number of different media and styles, which makes it difficult to generalize about their work. It aimed to provide a commercial enterprise, uniting artists with craftsmen, to create everyday items incorporating the ideals of the decorative arts. It was committed to functionalism and expressionism, and even before 1914 its artists were creating severe, unornamented pieces, which later found expression under the banner of Art Deco.

Silver

Much Wiener Werkstätte silverwork was made on a commission basis, so many pieces are one-offs. They were all

A silver bowl by Arthur Berger. c.1917 4.5in (11.5cm) diam E

handmade in the manner used by 18thC silversmiths – in contrast to Britain and the United States, where mass-production techniques were introduced during this period. Shapes borrowed from 18thC silver were very much in vogue; avant-garde pieces were made in relatively small quantities.

Marks

A rose mark was registered as a trademark in 1903, probably the same year that the Wiener Werkstätte monogram within an oval was registered as a hallmark.

Josef Hoffmann (Austrian, 1870–1956)

Hoffmann was one of the founder members of the Wiener Werkstätte. Although much of his work is in the severe style of the early 19thC, he produced pieces for the Wiener Werkstätte until the 1930s. His silverwork used smooth metal surfaces. He also designed jewellery, glassware, and furniture. His work often uses original and interesting shapes.

Dagobert Pêche (Austrian, 1887–1923)

Pêche joined the Wiener Werkstätte in 1915. His work has a strong organic emphasis and is relatively ornate and surfaces are very seldom plain. He also designed furniture, ceramics, glass, bookbinding, textiles, and wallpapers.

Georg Jensen

A Jensen silver and amber mounted box. c.1930 5.25in (13cm) high D

1. Is the surface fairly plain, without engraving or other decoration?
2. Are highlights (knops, feet, and so on) comparatively ornate?
3. Is the item high quality and obviously for the luxury market?
4. Is there a suggestion of Art Nouveau-style organic motifs, such as pods and tendrils?
5. Does the form exhibit a Neo-classical influence?
6. Does it have a highly polished finish?
7. Is the piece marked?

Georg Jensen (Danish, 1866–1935)

Jensen opened his first shop in Copenhagen in 1904 and soon had branches in Paris, London, New York, and other cities. With his partner Johan Rohde, he designed much of the firm's output but also employed several artists, notably Harald Nielsen from 1909 and, in the 1930s, Sigvard Bernadotte; the latter was responsible for many of the firm's linear incised engraved bodies. They made tea and coffee sets, candlesticks, cocktail shakers, tureens, cigar boxes, jewellery, and other items.

Decorative styles

Jensen's silver has some affinities with Arts and Crafts and Art Nouveau work, especially in its use of organic, pod, and tendril motifs and shapes. Elements are also borrowed from Neo-classicism and nature, combining to create a highly individual look that pioneered the Art Deco style in silver. Ornamentation tends to be restricted to features such as knops, feet, and handles. Geometric forms and motifs are avoided. Inset semi-precious stones are sometimes used.

Marks

Jensen pieces bear a variety of marks – usually, the guarantee of silver, the Jensen manufactory mark and maker's

A Jensen cocktail shaker by Harald Nielsen. c.1925 10in (25.5cm) high E

initials, and a shape number. Some pieces bear an importer's mark enabling them to be sold as silver outside Denmark. In Britain, pieces that do not bear this mark are designated "silver-coloured".

Marcel Wolfers (French, dates unknown)

Like Jensen, Marcel Wolfers concentrated on luxury items with simple, solid forms and spare decoration. His silver has a pronounced Modernist appearance, often emphasized by geometric motifs. He had a preference for combining different materials in one piece. His silver is always signed.

A silver Marcel Wolfers "Janine" service. c.1925 coffee pot 5.75in (14.5cm) high C

International Silver Company

A Gene Theobald for the International Silver Co., Wilcox Silver Plate Co.
four-piece tea set. c.1928 8.5in (21.5cm) E

1. Is it an example of industrial design?
2. Is it made of silver, silver plate, or pewter?
3. Is it machine-made and hand-finished?
4. Is it a piece of flatware or holloware designed for a hotel,
   institution, or steamship?
5. If a four-part tea service, does it fit neatly on a tray?
6. Is the piece marked by a designer or brand such as Wilcox Silver
   Plate Co. as well as International Silver Co.?

**International Silver Company
(American, 1898–1984)**

In 1898 a consortium of more than 30 small manufacturers of silver and plate combined to form one organization, the International Silver Company. Much of the commercial success was generated by the "Hotel Division", which specialized in flatware and holloware for use in hotels, institutions, and, during the 1930s, steamships. Many of these wares are of little collectable interest, but, during the 1920s and 1930s the company employed a number of outside designers, notably Donald Deskey, Kem Weber, and Gilbert Rohde, to design useful and decorative wares in silver, plate, and pewter.

Many pieces were produced through divisions that used older, prestigious trademarks such as the Wilcox Silver Plate Company; other names include Rogers, and Miller. All pieces bear the mark of the manufacturing company.

The International Silver Company's late 1920s designs include a series of four-part tea services such as this one (see left), designed by Gene Theobald. The pot, cream jug, and sugar bowl, all in electroplated nickel silver with Bakelite handles, sit in a tray. They are clearly machine-made, although they had to be finished by hand. They are representative of American silver plate of the time, which was heading away

from the European tradition, towards mass-produced industrial design.

Many items bear the signature of the designer and the company mark.

A silver-plated coffee set by Lurelle Guild for International Silver. c.1940 pot 12in (30.5cm) high D

A set of silver powder boxes by Eliel Saarinen for International Silver. 1934 5in (12.5cm) F

Cartier

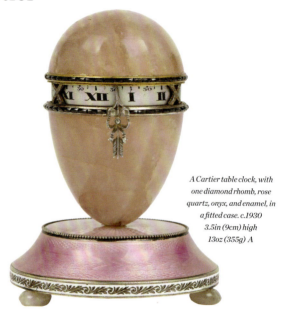

*A Cartier table clock, with
one diamond rhomb, rose
quartz, onyx, and enamel, in
a fitted case. c.1930
3.5in (9cm) high
13oz (355g) A*

1. Does the clock incorporate superb enamelwork or semi-precious stone inlay?
2. Are any metal mounts either gold or platinum?
3. Does the piece carry a serial number?
4. Is the appearance sculpted?
5. Does the clock show Oriental influences, using chinoiserie?

Cartier (French, 1898–present)

Cartier made a variety of timepieces, but favoured smaller forms such as desk and carriage clocks and the new wristwatches. Traditionally styled pieces continued to be made throughout the 1920s and 1930s, but more Modernist pieces were also made.

Clocks were treated almost as sculpture and their elaborate styling means that it is not always immediately apparent what their function is. Designs are often exotic or Oriental. Chinoiserie forms and decorative motifs with a Chinese influence are very common. Semi-precious stones are often embellished with fine-quality gems.

Jewellery

In the Art Deco period Cartier followed the fashion for contemporary shapes, embellishing them with large and colourful gemstones. Pieces were influenced strongly by Oriental, Egyptian, and Indian art. Cartier also produced jewelled luxury items, such as powder compacts and cigarette cases.

Cartier used jewels to dramatic effect, contrasting red or white against black, as in this onyx, coral, and diamond clip (see right) from c.1925. Pieces often make bold use of colour and shape, such as this tree brooch (see above right).

A Cartier onyx, coral, and diamond clip. c.1925 D

A Cartier ruby and diamond tree brooch. c.1930 2in (5.5cm) high A

183

Van Cleef & Arpels

*A Van Cleef & Arpels sapphire, diamond, and platinum
bar and ring brooch. c.1932 D*

1. Is the design inventive, using high-quality materials and
   settings (such as invisibly set stones)?
2. Is the design influenced by Persian, Oriental, or Medieval art?
3. Is it a plain design set with many gemstones?
4. Does it have a serial number?
5. Does the design incorporate geometric shapes and
   contrasting colours?
6. If a vanity case, is it a *minaudière* (a small, decorative
   evening purse)?

Van Cleef & Arpels (French, 1906–present)

Together with Cartier and Tiffany, jewellery produced by Van Cleef & Arpels belongs to the more opulent area of Art Deco design. The firm acquired a reputation for inventive luxury items, including a vanity case known as a *minaudière* ("simperer"), and a wide range of accessories influenced by Persian, Oriental, and Medieval art, using gemstones, enamels, and lacquer.

The company was happy to adopt the new design principles of geometric shapes and contrasting colours. Plain designs and shapes were employed as a foil for a profusion of gemstones rather than enamels and semi-precious stones.

- Innovative techniques included the invisible setting, a technique in which stones are fastened from the back, so it appears as though there is no metal mount.
- Van Cleef & Arpels pieces can be dated from their serial numbers.

Tiffany & Co. (American, 1837–present)

Tiffany created pieces for an elitist market, but the conservative tastes of rich America meant that there was very little demand for high-fashion jewellery. The new trends are more evident in the company's clocks. These often show a Chinese influence and make much use of precious stones, especially diamonds.

- Tiffany pieces are usually signed.
- The work of Tiffany & Co. should not be confused with that of Tiffany Studios, run by Louis Comfort Tiffany.

A Van Cleef & Arpels emerald and diamond bracelet, designed c.1922. A

A Tiffany Furnaces enamelled clock. c.1924 5.5in (14cm) high D

185

Gérard Sandoz

A French Gérard Sandoz shutter watch, sterling silver with eggshell and black geometric enamel decoration. c.1930 2.5in (6.5cm) wide D

1. Does the decoration contain geometric or Cubistic elements?
2. Is the form clean and simple?
3. Is there a contrast of colours?
4. Does the design suggest a machine influence, particularly in its use of contrasting metals and surface finishes for decorative impact?
5. Is the piece handmade?
6. Does the piece combine a number of different materials – for example, eggshell, silver, and lacquer? If jewellery, is there a combination of semi- or non-precious materials and stones?
7. Is the piece signed?

Gérard Sandoz (French, 1902–95)

Sandoz, who trained with his father Gustav Roger-Sandoz, is among the most inventive craftsmen of the Art Deco period, and one of the most commercial. He handmade small, individual luxury items, such as fine-quality lighters, boxes, and cigarette cases, as well as pendants and brooches, which belong almost exclusively to the 1920s. Unusually for work made for a luxury market, very little emphasis is placed on precious stones, although precious metals, such as gold, sometimes appear. Sandoz is particularly noted for his use of eggshell, lacquer, and niello work, and for his juxtaposition of materials and surfaces to give a textured effect.

Niello work

This term is used for silver and black lacquerwork, made by letting in thin lacquer onto a silver surface, which is then polished. Niello work was popularized in Russia in the 19thC and was favoured in Europe during the 1920s and 1930s.

Marks

Pieces are usually marked and may bear the signature of both father and son. Marks include "GERARD SANDOZ" and "Gérard Sandoz and G. Roger Sandoz".

Jean Goulden (French, 1878–1947)

Primarily an enameller, Jean Goulden produced table lamps, clocks, and other decorative items. Some of his designs were executed by Jean Dunand (see pp.24–5), from whom Goulden learned the craft of enamelling.

Most of Goulden's enamel designs were executed on silver or other precious metals, using the *champlevé* technique. He used areas of the base metal, in this case silver, as part of the decoration. Geometric patterns invariably dominate. Most of the items are signed.

Paul-Emile Brandt (Swiss, 1883–1952)

Brandt made small luxury items such as boxes, cigarette cases, and jewellery, especially bracelets and clips, many containing an element of lacquerwork. His designs of the 1920s and 1930s are strongly geometric, using materials such as gold and platinum combined with precious stones. Although similar to Sandoz's work, Brandt's pieces are often identifiable, not only by their use of precious stones but also by:

- the use of more clearly defined opposing areas of colour
- a strong symmetrical element
- a chevron motif
- the use of black enamel or onyx.

Jean Després (French, 1889–1980)

Després's work shows a Modernist, almost futuristic, approach, and makes very little use of gemstones, employing instead semi-precious stones and expensive metals. He concentrated on brooches and solid, chunky rings in abstract geometric patterns influenced by Cubism and African masks. His work is signed "J. Després".

Després generally avoided bright colours, preferring greys, blacks, and browns. Contrast is achieved through the use of strong relief elements, irregular surfaces, and patinations, as demonstrated in this 1930s brooch (see right).

Shapes as well as surfaces and colours were often contrasted: lines and curves may also be juxtaposed.

Many of Després's jewellery designs recall machine components. This brooch is typical, possibly inspired by his period in an aircraft factory during the First World War. Another of the designer's favourite technique was to set bloodstone against ivory and silver.

Raymond Templier (French, 1891–1968)

Another Parisian jeweller designing for the luxury market, Raymond Templier made brooches, pins, bangles, pendants, and earrings using geometric forms. Like Jean Fouquet (see opposite), he

A Després brooch for the Salon des Artistes décorateurs, Paris. 1932 1.5in (4cm) high C

used elongated forms in which circles are combined with verticals. Strong contrasts are achieved by the use of matt and polished surfaces.

White gold and platinum are contrasted with pavé set brilliants to produce a black and white effect; alternatively platinum is decorated with enamelled triangles.

La Maison Fouquet (French, 1862–1936)

Alphonse Fouquet (1828–1911) founded his company in Paris in 1862. His son Georges (1862–1957) joined the business in 1891 and took over when he retired in 1895.

Georges Fouquet

Georges designed both Art Nouveau and traditional jewellery before taking up the Art Deco style in the 1920s, and continued to work on individual commissions after the house closed due to bankruptcy in 1936.

Forms and styles

Fouquet's jewellery from the 1920s and 1930s is characterized by its use of combined precious and semi-precious materials. In the early 1920s he made mainly high-class pieces in the Parisian tradition, using diamonds and often exploiting the conflict of black and white. Later he became interested in hardstones, juxtaposed with more transparent precious stones, and he began to use semi-precious stones, such as rock crystal. Fouquet concentrated on making pendants, which are often multiple and use linked sections.

Marks

Pieces are usually signed "Fouquet" or "J. Fouquet".

A Jean Fouquet gold brooch with plique-a-jour enamel and diamonds. c.1950 2in (5cm) long D

Jean Fouquet

In 1919 Georges' son Jean (1899–1961) joined the firm and began to introduce geometric forms, some with Egyptian motifs. His work was exhibited at the 1925 Paris Exhibition.

After Maison Fouquet closed, Jean continued to design jewellery by outsourcing to other workshops. After the Second World War he worked on commissions for private clients from his apartment in Rue des Cerisoles. In 1952 he became a lecturer at the Ecole Nationale des Arts Decoratifs. Despite a serious illness he was able to exhibit a series of jewellery designs at the 1958 Brussels Exhibition.

Marks

Some pieces are signed "Jean Fouquet".

Other silver and jewellery

Although exclusive pieces use expensive jewels and materials and are signed by major artists, there are many other items available that, despite their use of less expensive materials and lack of a well-known signature, are well made and evocative of the time, and are therefore worth collecting.

As it became socially acceptable for women to wear make-up in public, the powder compact became popular. Handbags, which were considered an essential accessory, were narrow, so any accoutrements had to be slim and delicate.

There were many designs for dressing table sets, a medium that found fresh inspiration in the period. They are often made from silver and decorated with guilloché enamel.

A "Cube" tea set by Cube Teapots Leicester, UK. c.1920 4.5in (11.5cm) high F

- Sets are desirable. However, the brushes tend to need replacing relatively often and this is an expensive exercise, which deters some buyers.
- Sets should be complete, and are worth even more if other fittings are also included, such as a hair tidy, ring tree, candlesticks, powder box and cover, talc tube and cover, or matching jewellery box. Sometimes, especially if they are German, all these come in a fitted tray.

A number of "Cube" teapots were produced in silver and plate, especially in Birmingham and Sheffield. Art Deco tea and coffee sets sold well at the time they were made, as they were generally affordable to the general public. The minimum coffee set comprises a coffee pot, milk jug, and sugar bowl.

A 1930s enamelled compact, probably German. 3.5in (9cm) diam H

Many pieces were left undecorated, while others might feature a simple sunray motif.

Coffee sets often incorporated silver spoons with coffee bean terminals.

Watches with black shoelace straps are typical of the form and design popular in the 1920s and 1930s, and the best examples are set with diamonds, marcasite, or even paste stones.

Watches should be in working order. The strap need not be original.

Avant-garde watches and jewellery by top French designers were emulated by other makers. Fine-quality examples that use similar materials to those on good pieces – such as ivory and brilliant diamonds – may prove a better investment than an expensive signed piece, especially as new attributions are coming to light all the time.

Costume jewellery – pieces made

An English aquamarine-diamond pendant brooch. c.1920 2.5in (6.5cm) high C

from base materials, often in imitation of precious items – became highly fashionable in the 1930s as the Depression prevented people buying expensive pieces. Many designers who had worked for top jewellers such as Van Cleef & Arpels (see pp.184–5) found work with costume jewellery manufacturers. Names to look for include Trifari, Coro, Hobé, and Chanel.

An American watch brooch, set with onyx, emeralds, sapphires, and diamonds. c.1925 B

An Art Deco Bel Geddes for Trifari Jellybelly furclip. 1941 3.25in (8cm) high F

PRINTS AND POSTERS

In the 1920s and 1930s posters were used primarily as an advertising medium to promote travel, art exhibitions, and sports meetings, as well as occasionally for political propaganda. Poster designs of the period are unfussy, and the emphasis is on a strong central image. Colours were brighter than before, and new typefaces were employed.

The most striking images of the period are by French artists, the most innovative of whom was Cassandre (see pp.196–8), who used strong colours and an unusual sense of perspective. Paul Colin (see p.199) is the most important name in the area of theatre advertising, and is known for his posters featuring the actress Josephine Baker. Other major artists who worked on posters include Erté and Jean Dupas (see pp.200–1), many of whose lithographs have been converted into posters. Works by Icart were intended to be purely decorative: he produced no posters for advertising.

Travel posters focused on the possibility of speed that the new automobiles made possible. This French example (see opposite) by Roger Perot (1906–76) depicts the roadster on a sunny afternoon, with the car coming at the viewer at full speed, over a hill. The typography mirrors the angle of the car's front wheels. Similarly, in the Japanese railway poster (see p.194) designed by Munetsugu Satomi (1900–95), even the telephone poles bend to the train's speed and power. Unusually for a railway poster, the train itself is not depicted. Instead the poster gives a passenger's perspective of the train's speed.

In Britain, London Transport commissioned a series of posters from a number of leading artists. Subjects are often shown following the pursuits of the day, especially playing golf, and visiting places made more accessible by the railways – for example, seaside resorts. In the United States, Maxfield Parrish created posters reminiscent of the Art Nouveau style, but making use of more brilliant and unusual colours.

Film posters, now keenly contested by many poster collectors and film enthusiasts, are an area that grew with the development of Hollywood. They are in colour, often using two-tone artwork, and many are by unknown artists. Few have survived, although they were originally produced in large

"Delahaye" by Roger Perot.
1935 61in (155cm) high E

DELAHAYE

roger pérot '35

LES ATELIERS A.B.C., 52 Rue Mathurin Regnier, PARIS

numbers (every cinema would have had one).

Magazine covers and prints taken from magazines, described in some auction catalogues as "printed ephemera", are currently inexpensive. The original artwork is occasionally available, but is rare and usually commands a high price. Many European designers worked for American magazines such as *Harper's Bazaar* and *Vogue*.

Images were reproduced in a number of ways: collectors are likely to find references in auction house catalogues to posters, prints, lithographs, and drypoint and etching, and sometimes to the original artworks. Engraving is done with a knife straight onto the plate; in etching the plate is covered with wax, the design drawn into it, then the whole plate dipped in acid, which eats into the areas not covered by the wax. The result looks more like a drawing; engravings have a more stilted appearance, and an embossed effect. Lithographs are made by applying wax or an ink-resistant chemical to a stone surface, which is then covered with ink, so that exposed areas are coloured while others are left untouched. The ink lies on the surface which, unlike an etching, is completely flat. Photogravure is used to reproduce an etching or engraving: the item is photographed and the photographic negative applied to copper plate; the image is then etched or engraved. When photogravures are examined under a magnifier, the image is revealed as a matrix of tiny dots.

Prints and posters are not prone to being faked. Modern reproductions, which abound, are easy to detect as they are invariably executed on thicker paper with a glossy coated surface, and exhibit none of the characteristic signs of age of a 60- or 70-year-old work.

Condition is crucial to value. Pieces with tears and creases – especially those that interfere with the central image rather than the border – command a substantially reduced price, and unless the work is exceptionally rare, can be found at minimal cost. However, few posters from the period have survived completely undamaged as, not being intended as collectors' items, they were printed on poor-quality paper. The kinds of damage that are acceptable include minor fading or some loss of the paper around the edges. Some auction houses use letters to denote condition, ranging from "A" for those in very good condition, through to "D" for serious damage. Collectors prefer unmounted pictures; avoid those that have been applied to board.

"Japan", designed by Munetsugu Satomi. 1937 35in (89cm) high E

Adolphe Jean-Marie Cassandre

"Nord Express" by Cassandre. 1927 41.25in (105cm) high D

1. Is perspective used for dramatic effect?
2. Does the poster use shading to create an impression of movement?
3. Is it avant-garde, making use of strong images and bold lettering?
4. Does it show machinery of any kind?
5. Is the poster signed?

Adolphe Jean-Marie Cassandre (French, 1901–68)

Cassandre was born Jean-Marie Mouron in Ukraine, and as a young man moved to Paris. He adopted the pseudonym at the beginning of his career. He was one of the first to take up the language of formal art movements, such as Cubism and apply them to the more popular medium of the advertising poster. He is best known for his striking travel posters, many of which show ships and trains. Cassandre's work is often humorous and innovative.

The poster shown on the right is one of the first fashion advertising posters to show the direct influence of Cubism. The manner in which the legibility and message are achieved, through a strict geometrical approach tempered with shimmering airbrush treatment around the solid colours, became his signature.

Style and technique

Cassandre's distinctive graphic style uses strong, saturated colours combined with subtle shading to give subjects a sense of speed – a popular

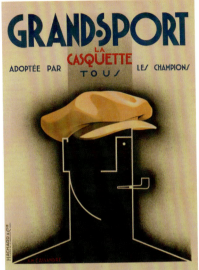

"Grand-Sport", designed by Cassandre. 1925 31.5in (80cm) high C

preoccupation during this period. His use of perspective is also distinctive and possibly shows a Japanese influence through simplification and elimination of superfluous details. Images are often stark and forceful: the poster shown left, celebrates the speed and modernity of the train, rather than emphasizing the luxurious aspects of rail travel.

Lettering is often bold, using clear type, usually sans serif, and Cassandre did not finish off the strokes of the letters with crosslines. The technical execution of the print tends to be masterful: surface brush or collage marks are usually invisible, and it is even difficult to distinguish hand lettering from type.

Collecting

Although Cassandre's work includes posters, lithographs, and cover designs for the magazine *Harper's Bazaar*, his original designs and drawings are not usually available. Even the posters are quite scarce. (In recent years they have most frequently been found in poster sales in New York.) Of his three best-known works, that advertising the liner SS *Normandie* commands a top price, followed by that for the Etoile du Nord railway service (see above), which uses an abstract interpretation of railway tracks to give a feeling of speed, space, and distance. The typography coralled at the bottom of the poster, and in a thin band around the border of the

A Cassandre "Etoile du Nord" poster. 1927 41in (104cm) high D

image, allows the motif of converging rails and a star representing the train on the horizon to dominate the page. This poster was revolutionary when it first appeared as it depicted no landscape, no destination, and no train. The low angle view of the rails is a signature technique of Cassandre's.

Colin went on to design hundreds of posters, stage sets, and costumes, easily keeping up with the furious pace of the Roaring Twenties! He was very fond of the piano as a decorative element, and it appeared in stylized forms in some of his earliest posters.

His first, and by far best, piano poster was for Wiener et Doucet in 1925, a perfectly soft, geometrically balanced poster. In 1927 he took the piano to further Cubist abstraction in an exquisite poster for Lisa Duncan. In 1929 he used this comfortable Cubist approach again for André Renaud (see left), a virtuoso who could play two pianos at the same time. Slightly more realistic and rigid than the two earlier posters, Colin still maintains a good and appealing stylized form.

His often light-hearted illustrative style is neither as austere nor as sophisticated as that of Cassandre. Nearly all of Colin's work features human figures, sometimes highly stylized, sometimes caricatured. His spirited, angular style epitomizes important aspects of the 1920s and 1930s poster.

Paul Colin (French, 1892–1985)

Like Cassandre, Colin designed travel posters, but his work also includes theatre programme covers and posters advertising performers as well as cigarettes and other products. In 1926 he opened the Ecole Paul Colin. He is best known for his posters to advertise visiting jazz musicians at the Folies Bergère. In just one night, in 1925, his poster for the Revue Nègre made Josephine Baker, jazz, and himself the craze of all Paris.

Jean Dupas

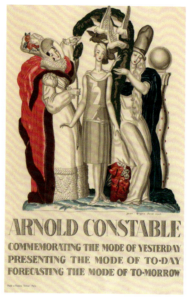

"Arnold Constable" poster for the New York department stores by Dupas. 1928 46.5in (118cm) high E

1. Are figures highly stylized, with elongated features?
2. Is the setting idyllic, possibly showing a Classical influence?
3. Are the colours relatively subdued?
4. Does the picture include animals?
5. Is any lettering separate from the image?
6. Is the work signed and dated?

Jean Dupas (French, 1882–1964)

Dupas was a painter and poster artist who trained at the major Paris schools. His work includes posters, catalogue covers, and large murals.

Dupas designed posters for a variety of clients. His work includes a series of advertisements for the American department store Saks Fifth Avenue and for London Transport, as well as fashion posters for Arnold Constable and others. There is also a series of posters advertising various public parks, including Hyde Park in London.

The advertising element is usually separated from the picture, and appears in simple lettering underneath in the manner of a slogan. Some works were not intended as advertisements but had the appropriate slogans added to them later.

Style

Dupas's pictures are characterized by their highly individual treatment of subjects, especially women, who are very idealized and rendered in highly decorative detail. Dupas tended to dehumanize his characters turning them into pretty, sharp-faced but sometimes expressionless mannequins. Women are always slender, willowy, demure, and young, with striking features – usually high foreheads with aquiline noses, and tranquil expressions. Colours are usually quite subdued. Foliage is also distinctive, with exaggerated towering trees and feather-like leaves.

Marks

Dupas's work is always dated and signed "Jean Dupas" at the bottom of the image.

Collecting

Dupas worked in a variety of media, including watercolours, pencil, and pastel on paper – which all tend to command higher prices than the posters. Oils in particular are usually very expensive. Some of the posters exist as limited edition lithographs.

"Bordeaux", designed by Dupas.
1937 39in (99cm) high E

Edward McKnight Kauffer

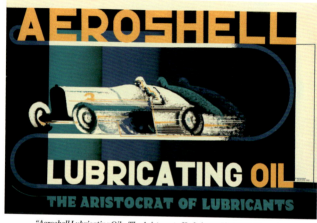

"Aeroshell Lubricating Oil – The Aristocrat of Lubricants" lithographic poster by McKnight Kauffer. 1932 29.75in (75.5cm) high D

1. Is the design strictly geometric or romantically soft?
2. Is it influenced by Futurism or Cubism?
3. Does it use bold colours?
4. Is there a sense of perspective?
5. Are the fonts used modern and simple?
6. Is the composition strong?
7. Does the design include abstract forms?
8. Does the poster advertise London Underground or an oil company?

202

"For Pull, Use Summer Shell" by McKnight Kauffer. 1930 45in (114.5cm) wide F

Edward McKnight Kauffer (American/British, 1890–1954)

McKnight Kauffer was born in the United States and arrived in Britain in 1914, having been encouraged to travel by a professor in Chicago named McKnight. He later took his name as a mark of respect. He is considered to be the leading British graphic artist of the era and was influenced by Futurism and Cubism. His best posters were designed for London Transport, British regional railway companies, BP, and Shell Oil. On his return to America in 1940 his clients included the New York city subway.

Depending on the campaign, McKnight Kauffer would alter his style from rigorous geometry to soft poetical illustration. This image (see opposite) combines both. It has a strong graphic construction, with the suggestion of a racecourse in the curvy lines that connect the text. The typography is geometric, but the car is treated more softly, with the illusion of speed created through the shadowy images behind it.

London Transport Posters

During the 1920s and 1930s London Underground commissioned posters from artists including McKnight Kauffer, Jean Dupas (see pp.200–1), Frank Brangwyn, and Rex Whistler. They use bold, highly legible typefaces and bright colours. They rarely show the method of transport, and concentrate instead on the destination. Many were inducements to leisure travel.

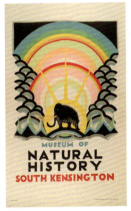

"Museum of Natural History" by McKnight Kauffer. 1923 38in (96.5cm) E

Jean Chassaing

A Chassaing poster depicting Josephine Baker.
1931 61.5in (156cm) high C

1. Is the face highly stylized?
2. Does the colour of the paper form part of the design?
3. Is the composition of the design accomplished?
4. Is it signed "J. Chassaing"?

A poster by Chassaing depicting the actress Janie Marèse. c.1928 63in (160cm) high E

Jean Chassaing (French, 1905–38)

Chassaing's first poster was published in 1923 and c.1925 he began working as an intern for Cassandre (see pp.196–8). There, he learned about composition and techniques such as airbrushing. In 1930 he founded Alliance Graphique. The way in which he depicted faces – particularly in his work after 1927 – shows the influence of Paul Colin (see p.199). There are only 11 known designs:

- c.1927: aeronautical posters for Pilotes d'Avion and Bernay.
- 1928: Janie Marèse. The only poster portrait of the actress who died in a car accident at the age of 23.
- c.1928: "Casino de la Mediterranée" and "Sardines" (only exist as maquettes).
- c.1930: La Regia, Kerlor, C'est un Amour Qui Passe, Le Blanc de Boka, and La Ligne Aurore (see below), for a line of women's shoes from Heyraud. It depicts a large shoe with a silhouette of a woman stretching over it to reach a line of shoes above.
- 1931: his best-known poster of Josephine Baker (see opposite), which features a highly stylized depiction of the dancer's face and in sections the colour of the paper is part of the design. It is considered to be his best image and was the one of which he was most proud.

Chassaing died prematurely and in poverty aged 33.

A Chassaing poster for La Ligne Aurore shoes. c.1930 63in (160cm) high F

Leslie Ragan

A Ragan poster featuring the Rockefeller Center. c.1936 40.5 in (103 cm) high C

1. Are bulky machines and buildings shown as objects of beauty?
2. Is light and shade used for dramatic effect?
3. Are clouds shown in great detail?
4. Is the text separate from the image?
5. Is the subject a train or cityscape?

Leslie Darrell Ragan (American, 1897–1972)

Leslie Ragan is best known for his paintings of trains and cityscapes, which he infused with light and enchantment. He was born in Woodbine, Iowa, and studied at Cumming School of Art in Des Moines, Iowa, and at the Art Institute of Chicago. Following military service he moved to California where he became a successful illustrator. His distinctive style transformed mundane, bulky machines and buildings into luminous, light-filled objects. Clouds of steam were painted with a spectrum of colour, rather than as simple white puffs with blue or grey shading.

His poster "Rockefeller Center, New York" (see opposite), depicts a bird's-eye view of the skyscraper rising up from the cityscape and put into monolithic perspective by St. Patrick's Cathedral in the foreground and the Hudson River and New Jersey in the distance.

One of the 20thC's most famous trains "The New 20th Century Limited" (see below) is a powerful Art Deco image that has been featured by the United States Postal Service on a series of stamps commemorating the 1930s, and is among the top American Art Deco posters ever designed.

"The New Empire State Express" by Ragan. 1941 40.75in (103.5cm) high D

"The New 20th Century Limited", designed by Ragan. 1938 40.75in (103.5cm) high B

Other prints and posters

Many other graphic designers – some unknown – contributed to the wealth of posters created in the 1920s and 1930s. Many show dramatic depictions of landmarks. Chesley Bonestell's poster for the New York Central Building (see below) features a dramatic evening scene of the building, which sits above Grand Central Station. It is framed

A poster by Simon Bussy, "Scotland by East Coast". 1927 40in (101.5cm) high E

A poster by Chesley Bonestell, "New York Central Building". 1930 40.5 in (103cm) high E

between the beams of two klieg lights and the buildings on Park Avenue.

Little is known about Simon Bussy who created this "Scotland By East Coast" poster for the London & North Eastern Railway (see above). It shows a stylized image of a fawn leaping through ferns. Bussy, along with Edward McKnight Kauffer (see pp.202–3), was connected to the Bloomsbury group of English writers and artists.

Many of the most charming graphics of the period are those with an element of humour, such as the one for Maurin Quina (see opposite above), which shows a green devil uncorking a bottle of its drink. The artist, Leonetto Cappiello, sets off the vibrant colours of the figure and text by placing them

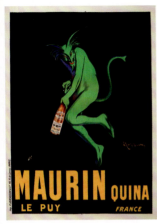

*"Maurin Quina", by Leonetto Cappiello.
1906 62.5in (159cm) high F*

1927 science fiction movie *Metropolis* (see p.210). It shows the film's central character, Maria, as a robot in an hypnotic image of stylized realism.

In contrast, Boris Lovet-Lorski's (1899–1973) poster "Mme. Anna Robénne / Russian Dancer" (see p. 211), combines abstract beams of light with the sensuous profile of the dancer, and gives her transparent veils a Cubist treatment. The geometric, red lettering stands out against the gradation of black, grey, and white in the background.

Weimer Pursell's dramatic poster against a plain, black background.

As drinking in public became more fashionable many drinks companies, notably Dubonnet in France, used Art Deco posters to advertise their products. Ernest Deutsch-Dryden (1883–1939) created this poster (see right) for the small champagne house Devaux. It plays with perspective, depicting a gentleman in tails, lighting a cigar in front of an oversized glass.

Werner Graul (1905–84) designed one of the most memorable posters of the Art Deco era – that for Fritz Lang's

"Champagne Devaux" by Ernest Deutsch-Dryden . 1938 61in (155cm) high E

*"Metropolis", by Werner Graul, advertising Fritz Lang's 1927
science fiction movie. 1926 27.25in (69cm) high A*

for the 1933 Chicago World's Fair (see below right) depicts the towers of the Federal Building jutting up into the text.

Loose fashion plates and magazines with colour illustrations probably provide the best opportunity for putting together a collection of Art Deco graphics at a low cost. Many are well executed and attractive but suffer in value because they are by an unknown artist. There is also growing interest in other printed ephemera such as cigarette cards and chocolate box covers. Avoid pictures that have been pasted on board as this affects the value adversely: ideally, they should be unmounted or at least mounted professionally, using acid-free boards.

"Mme. Anna Robénne / Russian Dancer", by Boris Lovet-Lorski. c.1925 80in (203cm) high D

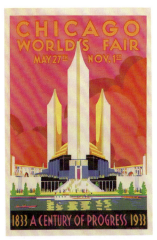

"Chicago World's Fair", by Weimer Pursell. c.1933 41.5in (105.5cm) high F

RUGS AND TEXTILES

In the early 20thC the rug enjoyed something of a revival in Britain. The role of the rug was re-evaluated: it was no longer merely a decorative floor cover unrelated to the decor and furnishings of the room, but was elevated to the status of a work of art. Decorative effect took precedence over considerations of utility and practicality. In Britain, a number of major designers, among them Frank Brangwyn, Marion Dorn, and her husband Edward McKnight Kauffer (see pp.202–3) were commissioned to design rugs.

During the 1920s and 1930s many rugs were also imported from Belgium. These often have abstract patterns and are usually in sombre colours. They tend to be symmetrical, made in two parts joined by a central seam. Most are by anonymous designers.

In France, as elsewhere, the best rugs of the period were commissioned, many for exhibitions or luxury liners. Many were made by the top designers of the day such as Jacques-Emile Ruhlmann (see pp.14–17), Paul Follot (see pp.18–21), Jean Lurcat, Jules Leleu, Süe et Mare (see pp.22-3). The Irish-born designer Eileen Gray (see pp.214–15) also created rugs for French clients.

In the United States, Ruth Reeves designed some rugs for W. & J. Sloane that evoked American city life (see below right), such as "Manhattan", as well as a series dominated by Cubist and geometric motifs. Top designers in other media also turned their attention to textiles – for example, Donald Deskey (see pp.34–6 and p.216), Gilbert Rohde, Eugene Schoen, and Loja Saarinen, who designed some rugs for the influential Cranbrook Academy.

Rugs were varied in shape, and no longer restricted to simple rectangles; some are round. Colours were no longer dark and sombre as they had been (presumably largely for practical reasons). Many rugs from the 1920s and 1930s are very pale, and tend towards autumnal and subdued tones of brown, green, black, grey, or delicate pastels. McKnight Kauffer's rugs, executed in bold primary colours, are exceptions.

Designers dispensed with fringing and borders, and with the symmetry that had dominated earlier designs. The pile is regular, as they are usually machine-woven, and the most common material is wool. They are often signed by the designer, which is rare in any other period. The wool is subject to fading, so strong colours are often at a premium.

*A geometric rug marked "GN" in the pile,
designed c.1930. 106in (270cm) wide D*

*A block-printed tapestry by Ruth Reeves, "The
American Scene". c.1930 83in (211cm) long D*

Eileen Gray

An Eileen Gray "Solidadi: Nude/Torso" rug. mid-1920s 125in (312.5cm) long F

1. Does the design use large geometric shapes?
2. Is it made from hand-knotted wool?
3. Does it use a limited, subdued colour palette?
4. Does the design include stylized flowers within a geometric border?
5. Is the surface textured?

Eileen Gray (Irish/French, 1878–1976)

Gray is one of the most influential designers of the early 20thC. She studied painting and went on to work as a lacquer artist, before becoming known for her furniture and architecture.

Rugs

In 1919 Gray completed her first overall interior design for an apartment in Paris. It contained geometric patterned rugs. In 1922, in collaboration with the architecture critic Jean Badovici, she opened the Galerie Jean Désert in Paris. The gallery sold rugs, furniture, and lighting.

Gray designed her rugs using gouache paint or making collages and they were handmade in a Paris workshop. She developed a hand-knotting technique that resulted in the creating of the first textured carpets. Earlier Gray rugs tend to feature geometric patterns – many are like abstract works of art. One was named "Ulysses", as a tribute to the Irish writer James Joyce, whom she knew. Others were named after places she visited such as "Saint Tropez" and "Castellar", but several had Irish names such as "Kilkenny" and "Wexford".

Reproductions

Many of her designs are now being reproduced. Reproductions are worth a fraction of the value of an original.

A late 1920s Eileen Gray Modernist wool rug. 114in (290cm) long E

Other rugs and textiles

Many textiles were designed by Donald Deskey (see pp.34–6), an American Modernist designer who created furniture and lighting from the 1920s to the 1940s, although most of the pieces on the market today date from the 1920s and 1930s. He is best known for the interior design of New York's Radio City Music Hall, which was completed in 1932. It became a New York City landmark in 1978, and a year later a major renovation began, partly funded by selling the original furnishings, which were replaced with reproductions. The carpets (see below) – which feature a

An Art Deco Egyptianesque carpet, designed c.1922. 179.5in (456cm) long G

patchwork of musical instruments – were made into rugs. They are marked "RADIO CITY MUSIC HALL". Deskey went on to design more textiles, many of which were used to decorate his room screens.

The fashion for Egyptian-inspired decorations extended to carpets (see above), which might feature motifs such as lotus flowers, scarabs, hieroglyphics, pylons, and pyramids either as an all-over design or simply used for the borders.

At the beginning of the 1920s, many French artists became fascinated by the potential of textile design and by the mid-1920s many were designing fabrics for upholstery and screens, as well as rugs and carpets. Among them were Edouard Bénédictus (1878–1930), Raoul Dufy (1877–1953), and Fernand

A Donald Deskey/Radio City Music Hall wool carpet. 1932 82in (208cm) long F

A wool art rug, after a design by Fernand Léger, designed c.1927. 65.5in (166.5cm) long D

A piece of gauze by Sonia Delauney, decorated with Cubist squares. c.1925 56.75in (144cm) wide G

Léger (1881–1955) who, like many of his contemporaries, also designed ballet sets and costumes. Léger was influenced by Cubism and went on to develop "machine art" – an abstract style that depicted monumental mechanistic forms in bold colours. This rug (see p.217, top) is typical of his abstract work.

Another artist who became well known for her Art Deco textiles was Sonia Delaunay (1885–1979). Born in Russia, she moved to Paris and married the French Cubist painter Robert Delauney (1885–1941). She designed graphics and sets for the Ballets Russes and by 1914 was creating Cubist fabrics in earth tones. This led to a line of Cubist-inspired fabrics (see p.217, bottom), throws, dresses, and men's clothes after 1914. Delauney was so successful she had her own pavilion at the 1925 Paris Exhibition. From the 1930s she mainly concentrated on painting.

Unsigned rugs from the 1920s and 1930s turn up fairly frequently at auction and many are surprisingly affordable. Contemporary catalogues and magazines show how important they were to the style of interiors at the time. They tend to be well made and solid, with a canvas backing, and were intended for use on floors rather than as wall hangings.

The most prized examples are those with Modernist or other avant-garde designs, especially if they were made in bright colours. Many less expensive examples are so because they are unsigned, or because they show excessive signs of

A 1930s wool area rug, with geometric pattern.
77in (195.5 cm) wide G

A pair of 1930s French geometric
bedside rugs. Each 52in (132cm)
wide E

decidedly Modernist in style,
and they are in still in good
condition. Because they are
unsigned they are likely to be
inexpensive and therefore
represent good value.

The bright colours of the
1920s gave way in the 1930s
to more subdued tones and a
greater interest in texture.

wear. Others misinterpret key elements
of the Art Deco style – for example, by
choosing colours
that are too dull (see
above) or clash with
each other, or by
crowding the design
with too many over-
elaborate patterns.

These art rugs
(see left and right),
with their bold
geometric designs
in tones of brown
and pink or blue,
and juxtaposition
of circles or squares
and stripes, are

A wool rug, with a stylized
pattern, unmarked. c.1932
53.5in (136cm) wide F

219

Glossary

acid-cutting method of decorating glass by which the objects are coated with wax or another acid-resistant substance, then incised with a fine steel point and dipped in acid.

acid-etching technique involving treatment of glass with hydrofluoric acid, giving a matt or frosted finish.

amboyna mottled, highly grained wood of an Indonesian tree.

Art Nouveau movement and style of decoration characterized by sinuous curves and flowing lines, asymmetry, and flower and leaf motifs, prevalent from the 1890s to c.1910.

Arts and Crafts Movement 19thC artistic movement, led by William Morris, which advocated a return to quality craftsmanship and simplicity of design in the face of mass-production.

Bakelite early form of plastic invented by L. H. Baekeland in 1909 and used to make a variety of domestic objects.

Bauhaus style German school of architecture and applied arts founded in 1919 by Walter Gropius. The Bauhaus style is characterized by austere, geometric forms and modern materials such as tubular steel.

cameo glass glass with two or more different-coloured layers, with a carved design in relief. The relief design is often finely engraved to add definition.

car mascot ornamental badge or device to be mounted on a car radiator cap.

chinoiserie decoration consisting of Oriental-style figures and motifs, such as pagodas, pavilions, birds, and lotus flowers, which permeated Europe from the Far East; prevalent from the late 17thC.

chryselephantine combination of ivory and a metal, usually bronze; used for Art Deco figures.

***cire perdue* (lost wax casting)** method of casting bronze or another metal in which a wax model is enclosed within a plaster mould, the wax is then heated and replaced with molten metal to form the object.

crackle glaze (craquelure) deliberate cracked effect achieved by firing ceramics to a precise temperature.

Cubism early 20thC art movement characterized by distortion, angularity, geometric arrangements, and features of African sculpture.

dinanderie work in non-precious metals.

etching type of engraving in which the design, drawn with an etching needle on a copper plate coated with an acid-resistant, is dipped in acid, then used to transfer ink to paper.

faïence French term for tin-glazed earthenware.

gesso plaster-like substance applied in thick layers to an inexpensive secondary timber before carving, gilding, and painting.

gouache opaque watercolour painting. Pigments are bound with glue.

guilloché enamel translucent enamelling, usually applied over an engraved or engine-turned metal base to create the shimmering effect of watered silk.

holloware hollow items such as bowls, teapots, and jugs; distinct from flatware.

intaglio incised design, as opposed to a design in relief.

ivorene worthless plastic substance resembling ivory.

lacquerwork layers of varnish prepared from the sap of the *Rhus vernicifera* tree, used as a ground for Oriental decoration. European imitations are known as "japanning" and vernis Martin.

limed oak oak coated with lime, which is then brushed off to leave a white residue in the grain.

lithograph method of polychrome printing in which a design is drawn in ink on a stone surface and transferred to paper. Lithographic prints were also used to decorate ceramics.

lustre ware pottery with an iridescent surface produced using metallic pigments, usually silver or copper.

macassar a rare form of ebony.

marquetry use of veneer and often other inlays to make decorative patterns in wood.

martelé French term for silverware with a fine, hammered surface first produced in France and revived by the American Gorham & Co. during the Art Nouveau period.

Modernism/functionalism style of the 1920s and 1930s inspired by a need to break with the past and to express the spirit of a new machine age. It rejected ornamentation in favour of geometric forms and smooth surfaces.

niello compound of silver, lead, copper, and sulphur applied to metal and fired to create a lustrous black surface.

opalescent translucent white glass; a reddish core is visible when held up to the light.

opaline glass translucent white (opalescent) glass made with oxides and bone ash. It reveals a red or yellow tint ("fire") when held up to the light.

ormolu ("gilt bronze") gilded, brass-like alloy of copper, zinc, and tin, used for mounts on fine furniture.

pâte-de-cristal almost transparent glass made of powdered glass paste that has fused in a mould.

pâte-de-verre ("glass paste") translucent glass created by melting and applying powdered glass in layers or by casting it in a mould.

patination alteration to the surface appearance of metal caused by time, use, or chemical corrosion.

pavé setting in jewellery; gemstones set so close together that no backing material is visible.

planished technique of producing a smooth finish on metalwork by gently hammering or rolling the surface.

plywood form of laminated wood with the grain of the alternate layers set at right angles.

pochoir reproduction process using different stencils for each colour of a print, applied over a black and white reproduction of the original.

Raku form of Japaense earthenware covered with a thick lead glaze.

sgraffito form of ceramic decoration incised through a coloured slip, revealing the ground beneath.

slipware type of red-bodied earthenware decorated largely with slip in contrasting colours.

spelter zinc alloy, an inexpensive alternative to bronze. Used in the production of figures.

streamlining style with flowing curved lines and aerodynamic form, prevalent in American design of the Art Deco period.

transfer-printing transfer of an inked image from an engraved plate to paper or to a sheet ("bat") of tacky glue and from there to a ceramic object.

wheel cutting/carving method of decorating glass by cutting it using a small rotating wheel fed with an abrasive.

woodcut print made by drawing the design on the surface of a block of wood and cutting away the parts to remain white in the picture. The surface is then inked and transferred to paper.

ziggurat stepped pyramid-shaped pedestal of marble or onyx for small bronze figures.

Index

Page numbers in *italic* refer to the illustrations

Acknowledgements

Alan Moss
436 Lafayette Street,
New York
NY 10003, USA
www.alanmossny.com
p.32, p.37br, p.213bl

Alfies Antiques Market
13–25 Church Street, London,
NW88DT
www.alfiesantiques.com
p.127br

Art Deco Etc
73 Upper Gloucester Road,
Brighton, BN1 3LQ, UK
johnclark@artdecoetc.co.uk
p.110, p.111

Ashmore and Burgess
10A Doddington Road,
Chatteris, PE16 6UA
www.ashmoreandburgess.com
p.76tl

Bloomsbury Auctions
Bloomsbury House,
24 Maddox Street, London, W1 S1PP
www.bloomsburyauctions.com
p.203tl, p.209tl, p.209br

Bonhams & Goodman
7 Anderson Street, Double Bay,
NSW 2028, Australia
www.bonhamsandgoodman.com.au
p.148

Bukowskis
Arsenalsgatan 4, Box 1754,
111 87 Stockholm, Sweden
www.bukowskis.se
p.73

Calderwood Gallery
631 North Broad Street,
Philadelphia, PA 19123, USA
www.calderwoodgallery.com
p.11, p.17, p.18, p.19br, p.21tr, p.23, p.166

Central Collectables
www.centralcollectables.com
p.112

David Pickup
115 High Street,
Burford, OX18 4RG
p.42

Decodame.com
853 Vanderbilt Beach Road,
PMB 8, Naples, FL 34108, USA
www.decodame.com
*p.56, p.77c, p.77br, p.88br, p.126tl, p.162,
p.181tr, p181br, p.186, p.191br, p.215, p.219tl*

Mallams
Bocardo House,
24a St Michaels' Street, Oxford,
OX1 2EB
www.mallams.co.uk
p.103

Moderne Gallery
111 North 3rd Street, Philadelphia,
PA 19106, USA
www.modernegallery.com
p.19t, p.20, p.21bl

Modernism Gallery
800 Douglas Road,
Suite 101, Coral Gables,
FL 33134, USA
www.modernism.com
p.30, p.33bl, p.33br, p.36b

Onslows
The Coach House, Manor Road,
Stourpaine, DT11 8TQ
www.onslows.co.uk
p.196

Pierre Bergé & Associés
92, avenue d'Léna,
75116 Paris, France
www.pba-auctions.com
p.88tl

Private Collections
*p.76br, p.96tl, p.96tr, p.99br, p.99tr, p.146,
p.154, p.155, p.191bl, p.198*

Quittenbaum
Hohenstaufenstraße 1,
D-80801 Munich,
Germany
www.quittenbaum.de
p.25, p.47, p.153, p.169bl, p.188

Rosebery's
74–76 Knight's Hill,
West Norwood,
London, SE27 0JD
www.roseberys.co.uk
p.100br, p.106, p.159tr

Rossini SA
7, rue Drouot, 75009 Paris,
France
www.rossini.fr
p.217b

David Rago Auctions
333 North Main Street, Lambertville,
NJ 08530, USA
www.ragoarts.com
*p.8bl, p.12, p.28, p.31, p.34, p.35, p.36tl, p.37tl,
p.38, p.44br, p.50, p.51, p.52, p.53, p.55tr,
p.58, p.63, p.66, p.67, p.75, p.82, p.86, p.87tr,
p.87br, p.89tl, p.90, p.91, p.124, p.125, p.161,
p.167, p.169tr, p.170, p.171bl, p.171tr, p.176,
p.180, p.213tl, p.214, p.216bl, p.217t, p.218,
p.219br*

The Silver Fund
www.thesilverfund.com
p.9tr, p.173t, p.179t

Skinner Inc.
The Heritage on the Garden,
63 Park Plaza,
Boston, MA 02116, USA
www.skinnerinc.com
p.26, p.83, p.104

Sotheby's
34–35 New Bond Street,
London, W1A 2AA
www.sothebys.com
p.15br, p.24, p.54, p.62, p.118bl, p.164

Sotheby's New York
1334 York Avenue,
New York,
NY 10021, USA
www.sothebys.com
p.134, p.139l, p.165

Swann Galleries
104 East 25th Street,
New York, NY 10010, USA
www.swanngalleries.com
*p.193, p.194, p.197, p.198, p.199, p.200, p.201,
p.202, p.203br, p.204, p.205tl, p.205br,
p.206, p.207bl, p.207br, p.208bl, p.208tr,
p.210, p.211bl, p.211br*

Sworders
14 Cambridge Road, Stansted Mountfitchet,
CM24 8BZ
www.sworder.co.uk
p.43, p.113, p.119bl, p.141, p.175

Tennants
The Auction Centre,
Harmby Road, Leyburn,
DL8 5SG
www.tennants.co.uk
p.133

Toovey's
Spring Gardens,
Washington,
RH20 3BS
www.tooveys.com
p.149br

Woolley and Wallis
51–61 Castle Street, Salisbury,
SP1 3SU
www.woolleyandwallis.co.uk
*p.1, p.41, p.55bl, p.69, p.70, p.89br, p.92, p.93,
p.94, p.98, p.100c, p.102, p.107, p.115, p.119tr,
p.126b, p.130, p.145, p.156*

Von Zezschwitz
Friedrichstrasse 1a,
D-80801 Munich, Germany
www.von-zezschwitz.de
p.135, p.138